THE BLIND BEAUTY

THE BLIND BEAUTY

A Play by

BORIS PASTERNAK

translated by
MAX HAYWARD and MANYA HARARI

With a Foreword by
MAX HAYWARD

Collins and Harvill Press
London, 1969

Printed in Great Britain by
Cox & Wyman Ltd, London, Fakenham and Reading.

FOREWORD

'I want the heart of the matter . . .
The meaning, cause,
Foundations, roots
And kernel
Of vanished days.'
(From: Poems, 1955–1959. Translated by Michael Harari.)

In the last year of his life Pasternak told several of his correspondents in the West about a play he was writing. He also read parts of it and described it to several people who visited him, at that time, at his home in Peredelkino, near Moscow. To the Swedish publisher of *Dr. Zhivago*, Mr. Georg Svensson, he wrote in September 1959 about an 'early rough draft' of a play whose action took place 'on the eve of the liberation of the peasants from servitude, about the year 1860', and which would feature 'serfs formed and brought up to [be] actors, artists in bondage,[1] family complications, duels, etc., etc.' He went on to say that he wished to portray all this in 'realistic verisimilitude', but that his main intention, as 'in the novel' (i.e. *Dr. Zhivago*), was to 'give . . . a conception of life in general, of life as such, of historical being or existence'. The play, with its 19th century setting, was thus at least in part conceived as a pretext for another endeavour to get 'to the heart of the matter'.

In a letter of November 14, 1959 to a French friend, Jacqueline de Proyart, he wrote that *The Blind Beauty* (as the play was to be called), if he lived long enough to finish it, would be as vast in its sweep and cast of characters as *Dr. Zhivago*, by which it had been 'anticipated' and which he hoped it would 'continue and deepen'. In December 1959, he again wrote to Madame de Proyart to say, with reference to

[1] The letter is in Pasternak's vivid but faulty English, and by this expression he was probably trying to translate the Russian word for 'serf actors'.

The Blind Beauty, that he wished to make one more painful effort to 'leap forward, get away from the ground, from the present, to seize a small part of that obscure and magic thing called destiny, the future'.[1]

In January 1960 he was visited in Peredelkino by Mrs. Olga Carlisle, the grand-daughter of the novelist Leonid Andreyev, to whom he gave a detailed description of the play, reproduced in her book *Voices in the Snow*.[2] Pasternak told her that the play was a trilogy, of which the first two sections had already been partly written. The third part, however, so far existed only as a rough draft. In a letter to George Reavey dated February 7, 1960 he said: 'after to-morrow I shall return to my poor play that I have abandoned half a month ago.'[3]

In April of the same year Pasternak fell seriously ill, and on May 31st he died.

Assuming that the three parts were of similar length,[4] he was able to complete something between a half and two thirds of the play. The first part, called the Prologue, is divided into two scenes. The first scene takes place in the house of the estate of Pyatibratskoye in October 1835, and the second, fifteen years later in a forester's hut on the same estate. The first act, described as the 'middle part of the drama" is also divided into two scenes – the first in a peasant's house on the estate, and the second in the waiting room of a posting station nearby. The time of the first act is about 1860.

---

[1] Jacqueline de Proyart, *Pasternak*, Paris 1964, page 39. In Pasternak's original French this passage reads: 'Il faut que je fasse encore une fois cet effort pénible, que je m'arrache au sol, au présent, que je m'élance en avant, que je gagne de nouveau un morceau, une portion de cette chose magique et obscure: du destin du futur.'

[2] London, 1963, pp. 201–8. This account does not correspond in all particulars to the play as we now have it – Pasternak must subsequently have changed his design in some details – but it is invaluable as the only published description of the unwritten part.

[3] Harvard University Library Bulletin, Volume 15, no. 4.

[4] Pasternak used the word trilogy only to Mrs. Carlisle; to his other correspondants he spoke in terms of a single play (evidently divided into three parts: a prologue followed by two acts) which he hoped, despite its length, it would be possible to perform in a single evening.

The Prologue deftly conveys the quality of life in the Russia of Nicholas I. Ten years after the crushing of the Decembrist revolt, serfdom seems the natural condition of man, peasants are taken from their wives and children to do military service for 25 years (the master and mistress of Pyatibratskoye, at the beginning of the play, have gone away, not to hear the sobbing of the women as recruits from their estate are handed over to the army), minor disobedience is punished by flogging in the stables and major offences by being made to run the gauntlet between two rows of soldiers armed with sticks (the so-called 'green road'). But there is unrest and already a menacing hint of change in the air: the forests are full of bandits, run-away serfs and conscripts; there are cases of mutiny in the 'military settlements';[1] many of the landed estates, as in the play, are heavily mortgaged and on the verge of ruin, the owners are dispirited, and some of them are inclined to fantasies about improving their fortunes by emancipating their serfs. The present is haunted by memories of an even more oppressive past – the servants in the play tell stories about Domna the Murderess, the great-grandmother of the Count, who did nearly a hundred and fifty of her serfs to death, and whose fancy dress with a painted cat-fish mask, still kept in the house, plays a fateful part.[2] There are ominous signs and portents: it is said that when the plaster bust of an unknown young man in the Count's study is broken, then the estate will be ruined. The bust is indeed smashed by a bullet during a shooting match between the Count and his valet, who is the Countess's lover. The same shot blinds Lusha, a beautiful serf girl. Of this figure in the play, Pasternak said to Mrs. Carlisle that she is 'of course symbolic of Russia, oblivious for so

[1] These were military – agricultural communities set up under Alexander I to strengthen internal security and eventually intended to replace the conscript army; they consisted of state peasants who lived in barracks with their families and whose sons, too, were brought up as soldiers. The draconian regime in the settlements led to unrest at the end of Alexander's reign and at the beginning of Nicholas I's. The mutiny described in *The Blind Beauty* is clearly based on the uprising at Staraya Russa in 1831.

[2] The portrait of Domna is suggested by a historical figure, the infamous D.N. Saltykova (1730–1801) who, after murdering a hundred and thirty-nine of her serfs, fell foul of Catherine the Great and was imprisoned in a convent.

long of its own beauty, of its own destinies'. In what we have of the
play, however, this symbolism is not elaborated and Lusha remains
an episodic figure.

In the second scene of the Prologue, fifteen years later, we learn
that the Count had died after the melodramatic events of the first
scene, and that the Countess has married Iriney, his nephew and
heir, a liberal-minded person who would gladly emancipate his serfs
if it were technically possible and who is passionately devoted to the
arts. Like several great Russian landowners in the 18th and 19th
centuries (e.g. the Yusupovs in Petersburg and the Sheremetyevs at
Ostankino, near Moscow) he has his own troupe of serf actors, some
of whom he has sent to Paris for training. The best of them, Agafonov,
is the Countess's illegitimate son by her late husband's valet (who
had fled abroad after the shooting incident and taken service in
Sweden). Agafonov has been brought up as a serf by the blind Lusha
and is ignorant of his true parentage.

In the first act (the second part) we move on to 1860 – five years
after the death of Nicholas I and four years after the end of the
Crimean War. Reform and the emancipation of the serfs are not far
away. Russia is about to be swept forward into its modern age of
revolutionary movements and social transformations that will cul-
minate in October 1917. The play's cast of characters is an almost
complete range of the social types who will dominate the scene in
the future: Sasha, tutor to the new Count's children, a secret revolutionary and a future terrorist, the Count himself, a liberal who is
helping to prepare the Emancipation; Prokhor, the old Count's
butler, who had been sent to Siberia (via the 'green road') on a false
charge of shooting and wounding the Count and stealing the
Countess's diamonds, but who has now been rehabilitated to become
a thriving innkeeper, a good specimen of the energetic peasant type
that will form Russia's commercial and industrial class in the second
half of the century; finally, there is Straton, the local chief of police,
also of peasant stock, but a brutal upstart and vulgarian intended to
typify the worst kind of Tsarist officialdom that in the coming years
would try to contain the new social forces and thus greatly increase
their explosive power. By the convenient device of bringing to-

gether some of these personages with Alexandre Dumas[1] who is snowed up at a posting station on his way to see a performance in the serf theatre at Pyatibratskoye, Pasternak is able to give a superbly concentrated survey of Russia's mood and atmosphere on the eve of the Great Reforms.

The text as we have it ends with this encounter between Dumas and other characters, and it seems that Pasternak did not have time before his death to write down any more, except possibly in rough drafts that are not yet available. According to the account he gave Mrs. Carlisle, the second part of the trilogy would have continued with 'a play within a play' (as in Hamlet), which he intended to write in the style of a popular, mid-19th century melodrama. Before the performance of the play (entitled *The Suicide*) there was to have been a discussion on the nature of art between Dumas and the serf actor Agafonov which would have given Pasternak an opportunity to outline his own views on the subject. The first act was to have ended in a violent scene during which Straton, the police chief, would try to rape one of the serf actresses; Agafonov, in defending her, would strike her attacker with a bottle of champagne and would only be rescued from the consequences by the Count who arranges for him to go once more to Paris where he had been trained as an actor.

In the third and unwritten part, Agafonov would have returned to Russia to settle in the Petersburg of the 1880s as a successful actor – no longer, of course, a serf. In the end, developing the symbolism of the play's title, Agafonov would have brought a famous doctor from Europe to cure his foster mother, Lusha, of her blindness. Most interesting of all, in the final part of the play, would have been the figure of Prokhor. In the words of Pasternak to Mrs. Carlisle:

'In this part, Prokhor is an affluent merchant. I want to represent the middle class which did so much for Russia at the end of the 19th century. Imagine somebody like Shchukin, who collected

[1] It is a historical fact that Dumas (Père) travelled to Russia in 1858. His book 'Impressions d'un Voyage en Russie: de Paris à Astracan' was published in 1859.

all those beautiful French paintings in Moscow at the turn of the century.'

In giving this account of the play, as he saw it at the time of his meeting with Mrs. Carlisle, Pasternak several times made a highly significant comparison with Gogol's *Dead Souls*, saying, for instance, that in the first part (i.e. the Prologue) he had wanted to describe Russian life 'at its rawest, most trivial, in the manner of the first part of *Dead Souls* . . . before it has been touched by any form of spirituality.' This remark shows us very clearly what his intentions were, how closely they resembled those of *Dr. Zhivago*, and the meaning of his words to Jacqueline de Proyart that the play would 'continue and deepen' the novel. The first part of *Dead Souls* (published in 1841) was for its author a kind of descent into the Inferno of pre-Reform Russia, in which tyranny, corruption and ignorance were so unrelieved as to make one despair of humanity. Until his death in 1852 Gogol vainly tried to write a second part in which he wanted to show the light of possible future redemption already glimmering in the darkness of the present. But Gogol believed this could only come through a moral regeneration of which he saw so little actual sign among his countrymen that he ultimately despaired and burnt his draft of the novel's second part. Pasternak also believed in redemption, but of a kind in which he was able to retain his faith while living through an even darker historical period than ever Gogol could have imagined in his worst dreams. It was a faith based on a conception of life, formed already before the Revolution, that was to make him spiritually immune to the blandishments and the terrors of his age, and which perhaps sustained him through them, giving him the strength to survive and bear witness. He first outlined this conception in an essay published in 1916, *The Black Chalice*, where he gave it as his belief that there are two orders of reality, two universes which, though touching on each other, are nevertheless separate. The first and higher order is that which exists in eternity and is represented by poetry (or art), through which it may be glimpsed. The second and lower reality is that which we call by the name 'history', and which exists only in time. In this scheme of things there is a dialectical opposition between eternity and time, between poetry and history, between the artist and the 'man of action'. Seen in this light, the doings of men are ultimately contained within and subordinate to an infinite and eternal being (of which art and nature are manifestations) which may give grace to human activity or even redeem it. It is only awareness of the higher level of being, and the possibility of grace offered by it, that makes history bearable.[1] Pasternak saw the artist as one who was vouchsafed glimpses of eternal harmony and hence an agent of redemption. In a famous line he spoke of the poet as 'eternity's hostage to time' (*vechnosti zalozhnik u vremeni v plenu*), a definition which implies inevitable conflict between the artist and 'history'. Agafonov in *The Blind Beauty* like Dr. Zhivago, is at odds with his society – yet he is a product of it and represents in the last resort its only link with the eternity that enfolds and transcends it. The eternal, made manifest in art, is always present in the temporal, even at its most abject, and in the most hopeless periods of history there is thus a hint of redemption.

The significance of the former serf, Prokhor, passing through an abyss of humiliation to become eventually a patron of the arts is hence apparent as is the healing of the 'blind beauty' through the agency of her adopted son, the former serf actor.

The thematic links between *The Blind Beauty* and *Dr. Zhivago* are also evident in the light of Pasternak's general philosophy of history. He was fascinated by history as a symbol (in a poem from the Zhivago cycle, 'Garden of Gethsemane', he speaks of the passage of the ages being like a parable that 'catches fire on its way'). Russian history of the 19th century and in Pasternak's lifetime seemed to him to illustrate with particular intensity and drama the conflict between the two intersecting planes of reality, as he conceived them. Yet he was concerned to show in this play, as well as in his novel, that the history in which we are trapped is only a mirage, always about to dissolve into another one. Perhaps Russian history is particularly

[1] I am indebted for this interpretation to the remarkable essay on Pasternak by Andre Sinyavsky, who is still serving his sentence in a Soviet Labour Camp (see Boris Pasternak *Poems,* Moscow and Leningrad 1965).

suggestive in this sense. Russia is for ever 'on the eve' of great change: as in *The Blind Beauty*, an apparently stable reality may dramatically disintegrate, like the plaster bust in the Count's study, and new social configurations, already latent in the present, arise with particular suddenness to destroy the old, apparently immutable hierarchies. But, in Pasternak's view, all such tracings in the sands of history belonged to a transient and lower order of being which only art could endow with any sense of permanence or value. It was Pasternak's firm conviction that the artist can 'overcome' history. This is what he meant by saying in his letter to Jacqueline de Proyart that his historical play was a painful effort to 'leap forward, to seize a small part of that obscure and magic thing called destiny, or the future'.

St. Antony's College,
Oxford.
March 1969.

LIST OF CHARACTERS

*

Characters in order of their appearance:

CHRISTIAN FRANTSEVICH, estate manager
GIDEON, estate mechanic
PROKHOR DENISOVICH MEDVEDEV, butler
LUSHA, maid
MISHKA, houseboy
GLASHA, maid
SIDOR, floor polisher
FEDOSEY DULYCH, footman
PLATON SHCHEGLOV, valet, later Lieutenant Rimmars
ELENA ARTEMYEVNA SUMTSOV, married to Count Norovtsev
MAXIMILIAN (MAX) NOROVTSEV, Count,
    owner of Pyatibratskoye
KOSTYGA, highwayman
LYOSHKA LESHAKOV, highwayman
PAKHOM SUREPYEV, Lusha's father
MARFA, his wife
FROL DRYAGIN, stable boy
STRATON SILANTYEVICH NALYOTOV, policeman
SHOKHIN, gendarme
ALEXANDER SASHA GIDEONOVICH VETKHOPESHCHERNIKOV,
    Gideon's son, tutor to the Norovtsev children
ALEXANDRE DUMAS PÈRE, French writer
SELIVERST KUBYNKO, station master
KSENOFONT NOROVTSEV, distant relation of Count Max
NIKOLAY (KOLYA) CHERNOUSOV, Ensign
YEVSEY, young serf belonging to Ksenofont
MAVRA, beggar

GURY, beggar
YEVSTIGNEY KORTOMSKY, landowner
OBLEPIKHIN, General
OLEG ALEXANDROVICH, Grand Duke.

PROLOGUE

*

SCENE ONE

The study in Count Norovtsev's house in Pyatibratskoye in the eighteen thirties. The end of a grey October day. The room has four windows. There are several tables, armchairs, a sofa, a book-case. A big cupboard blocks the door into a corridor which is no longer in use. On top of the cupboard stands a large plaster bust of a young man wearing a wig of the period of Catherine II.

Enter the estate manager, CHRISTIAN FRANTSEVICH, *and the estate mechanic* GIDEON.

CHRISTIAN

Where the devil have they all got to? Oh, yes, they're beating the carpets outside. Well, what's that money you were grumbling about?

GIDEON

I was saying that I've had a lot of trouble with that mill. You owe me for the repairs. I know there's not a penny in the estate office. That's why I'm asking for a loan – I'll pay it back.

CHRISTIAN

You don't know what you're talking about. And you're blind drunk from early morning on! There's no money in the estate, and you want a loan! As if a loan weren't money, as if it were oats, or cabbage or something! Wait. There's that dog, Khort. He'll leave dirty paw marks, and the floor has just been polished. He's not to be let in. Get rid of him for Christ's sake. He frightens me.

A dog barks off-stage. GIDEON *walks to the door on the right.*

GIDEON

(*talking to the dog outside*): Back, Khort, back! You can't come in. Instead of scampering about clean floors, you ought to be tracking down that bandit, Lyoshka Leshakov.

GIDEON *returns to his place.*

CHRISTIAN

You'll never let me forget Lyoshka, will you? Can't you get it into your head once and for all that it wasn't we who had him flogged? He'd been conscripted. He was under the army's jurisdiction, not ours.

GIDEON

They dragged him past here, bound hand and foot. He had no breath or strength left even to groan, he was whimpering like a puppy. What do you expect the serfs to do except run away and join the highwaymen?

CHRISTIAN

What are you looking at over there?

GIDEON

That head on top of the cupboard – it's not in the middle. I'll get up on a chair and put it straight.

CHRISTIAN

Don't you dare touch it, drunk as you are. You try and keep your own head straight. Blind drunk from early morning on, that's what you are.

GIDEON

He was a handsome devil, too. But who he was, nobody knows.
Yet there are plenty of people on the estate who look like him –
the master for one, and his man Shcheglov. No wonder you
can't always tell them apart. Then there's no end of men and
women in the villages – who look just the same. A whole tribe,
all cast from the same mould. Who could that curly-headed
rascal have been, I wonder? It's a real mystery.

CHRISTIAN

That's a mystery you'd much better leave alone.

GIDEON

I know what you're going to say now. There's a superstition
that if ever that bust gets broken, it will mean the end of the
estate. But the estate is done for anyway, even though nobody's
ever so much as laid a finger on the bust.

CHRISTIAN

It's true, it's all going to ruin, all hanging by a thread. Land,
woods, buildings, everything down to the last stick of furniture,
all mortgaged and under restraint. Any day the whole lot will
be up for auction.

GIDEON

And you still wonder why I take to drink and ask for money?

CHRISTIAN

What business is it of yours?

GIDEON

Do you think it's easy for me to stand by and see everything go
to rack and ruin? That Herod with his fits and his twitching

B

arm, he's squandered his own fortune, and he's wasted all she had at Sumtsovo, and now he's trying to get hold of her diamonds as well!

CHRISTIAN

They're not your diamonds.

GIDEON

And what about my childhood memories? Do you think they count for nothing? My father said the liturgy at the chapel in the big house. When I was studying to be a priest, I used to spend my holidays at Sumtsovo. I used to pick mushrooms and berries in the woods with Elena.

CHRISTIAN

She had no lack of playmates in those days.

GIDEON

Just what do you mean by that?

CHRISTIAN

Well, there was Platon Shcheglov for one, a pretty boy in his Circassian coat. He was given her as part of her dowry and sent here with her to Pyatibratskoye.

GIDEON

Come on, out with it – what do you mean?

CHRISTIAN

Nothing special.

GIDEON

Just as well, or I'd have bashed your ugly face in. What do you think it's like for me to hear every Tom, Dick and Harry gossiping about them?

CHRISTIAN

Mind you don't start more gossip yourself while you're complaining of other people gossiping. Honestly, every free man on the estate ought to run away. It's like living on a volcano. Look at Khort, a creature without reason, a dog, not a human being, yet even he is restless, wandering about like a lost soul. He feels there's something in the air, dumb animal though he is.

GIDEON

An animal can feel. It's you who are an unfeeling brute.

CHRISTIAN

I'm not giving you any money, it's no good your asking. Meanwhile, here I am talking to you and forgetting what I came for. They're taking their time over cleaning the house, I'll have to shake them up. The master and mistress have sent word not to expect them for another three days. That means they'll come bursting in on us in about three hours, just to catch us on the wrong foot, to show that they keep their eye on things. That's why I've started all this commotion. The reason they rushed off was to be away while the conscripts were leaving, not to hear the women sobbing. Now the recruits are gone, they're coming back. But I've got more important business to see to than welcoming them home. I've got to send the grain carts off to town. They should have been well on their way by now, but they're still not past the gates. And look at how overcast the sky is. The nights are drawing in already. You'll see, we're sure to have rain or snow. Wet weather will ruin the grain. Or else Kostyga and Lyoshka will waylay the carts in Prince's Wood, and people will start saying it was all my fault – I put off sending them until nightfall because I'm hand in glove with the bandits. Come to think of it, there's a rumour going round about you – that when you repaired the mill for the master, you put up another in the ravine for the robbers.

GIDEON

You dirty miser! It's not enough that you grudge me a few score roubles, d'you have to start lying rumours about me as well?

CHRISTIAN

The world is full of rumours. I pass them on to you for what they're worth. But that isn't what I meant to tell you. The recruits have been gone for more than a week, but the peasants are still glowering like wild beasts. The carts should have been on their way long ago, but they've still not set off. So I went to the barn. Agafonov, Surepyev and the rest were there, loading and tying on the sacks. How much longer will you be, I said to them. Look at the weather, I said. Any moment it will rain or snow. Well, what d'you think? All they did was scowl at me, no one said a word – just as though I hadn't spoken to them. They're not afraid of the whip any more.

GIDEON

What did you expect them to do? Sing and dance for you? What have they got to be pleased about? The young men were all married off, and now that all the wives are with child, away they go to serve in the army for twenty-five years!

CHRISTIAN

I've told the Count over and over: sell Pyatibratskoye while there's still time, and transfer the peasants to the lands around Samara. Now it's too late. The property is mortgaged, the creditors are watching it. And in the state it's in, nobody would take it even if you gave it away. And just look what's going on in the neighbourhood! What about that? A stone's throw away, gangs of prisoners are driven along the highway to Siberia. The woods are full of run-aways, bandits are swarming all around. And the military settlements! I could tell you a thing or two about those that would make your blood run cold.

GIDEON

Really! Make my blood run cold, indeed. You miserly devil.

CHRISTIAN

It would make your hair stand on end. Listen to this. When I looked around and saw that the peasants were not to be relied on, I said to myself: I'll send a trusty man over to Straton Silantyevich Nalyotov, so that if the worst comes to the worst, at least we can be sure of getting help from the police. Well, the man comes back and reports. Not a soul in the camp – nothing but women left. And the women just laughed at him. A platoon of soldiers on the estate, is that all you want, they said. Haven't you heard? In all the military settlements in the district the men have mutinied. The officers are all away, dashing about from place to place. It's been a hot summer: cholera weather. In the camps they began putting lime into the water. It doesn't take much for ignorant people to get scared. The men started shouting that the doctors were murderers, they were poisoning the water, they meant to kill everybody. So they got together, tore the hospital orderlies limb from limb, and wrecked the barracks; the NCO's were all wiped out... Ah! Here they come, our dear ones!

> *Enter* LUSHA *and* GLASHA – *maids, both married and both in the family way;* MISHKA, *a houseboy; the butler* PROKHOR, *and* SIDOR, *the floor-polisher, carrying clean carpets, and curtains.*

I thought you were all dead, you lop-eared oafs. Here I come, sure that everything would be clean and polished, the study shining like a mirror – and you've done nothing but stand around yawning and loafing. Then you wonder why you get sent to the stables to be whipped.

PROKHOR

You should have a heart, Sir. We've all been on our feet since dawn. Think of what it means to clean a house like this down to the last pin! And both the women are with child. And on top of that, Khort, the Count's dog, puts his muzzle into everything and gets in our way when we're trying to shake the carpets! Anyway, what's the hurry? There's very little left to do. Don't let it worry you, Sir. Only the carpets to lay and the curtains to hang – we'll get it done in no time.

CHRISTIAN

All right, then this is how we'll do it. I've got to go off to the office, to make out the loading bills for the carts. Meanwhile, you get on with it, and see there's not a speck of dust left by the time I come back – I want everything to be bright as a new pin. And should they arrive in the middle of all this confusion, before I'm back, send Mishka instantly to the servants' hall, to tell them all to come and sing a welcome for the master and mistress, and mind you let me know at once. Come along, Gideon.

LUSHA

Beg pardon, your honour, but may I tell you something? Just now, when we were passing through the mistress's rooms, I noticed that the drawer of her desk – the secret drawer on the left hand side – was open about an inch, and the key was in the lock – just fancy such a thing! It's never happened before, she's never left it open like that. I hope it doesn't mean something bad! I pushed it in and locked it and took the key. Here it is. Would you take charge of it, please.

CHRISTIAN

And what the devil am I to do with it? You noticed something was wrong, you keep the key. Her ladyship didn't leave an inventory of her jewels with me. Come on, Gideon.

Exit. With MISHKA'S *help,* PROKHOR *leans a ladder against one window after another, and hangs the curtains.* SIDOR *polishes the as yet unpolished corners of the parquet floor. The women lay the carpets, dust the furniture, and the ornaments on the tables and shelves.*

PROKHOR

(from the top of the ladder): That's him all over! He's a good one for telling us off and threatening us with the whip, but when it comes to answering for something – oh no! not him – he clears off as fast as he can go! His heart's in his boots! . . . That's not the way, you're not laying the carpet right, women! That red Bokhara goes lengthways, in line with the pattern on the parquet. You've laid it crossways! How does the curtain hang, Mishka? Have a look from down there.

MISHKA

It's crooked, Uncle Prokhor, the pelmet's got its right ear hanging too low down. Pull it up a bit. Nail the fringe up on the right. Would his lordship really be so bold as to make you take your trousers down in the stables? Pull it up a bit more. Still more. Just a bit more. That's enough. Stop.

PROKHOR

What's it like now?

MISHKA

It's all right.

PROKHOR

No, my boy, it's only milkmaids and kitchen boys they whip in the stables. We butlers, footmen and the like get dressed up in tail coats and sent off to town, to the police station, with a note for the officer in charge: 'How are you, dear Straton Silantyevich? Why haven't we seen you for such a long time? I'm displeased with the bearer of this note, my outrider Fyodor. Do something, will you?' He makes the note out letter by letter, then he starts on you with his fists, and the soldiers beat you with sticks. Have a look. Is the fringe all right now?

MISHKA

Quite right. You can go on to the next.

GLASHA

The carpets are laid, Prokhor Denisovich. What are we to do next? We started dusting, but you told us off.

PROKHOR

That was before. Now the carpets have been laid, you can go over everything with a cloth. It won't get dusty again. Who's ever heard of starting with the dusting?

MISHKA

Wait, wait, Prokhor, look what you are doing. You've pushed the pelmet up too far. Pull it down on the right. More, still more. Is it true what they're saying that the robber chief Kostyga is in league with our peasants? They say he came up to Agafonov and Surepyev and the woodcutters while they were felling timber in Prince's Wood. He sprang up in front of them right out of the ground to make a bargain with them.

PROKHOR

How am I to put some sense into you, you chatterbox. Shouting about things like that at the top of your voice! It's all lies . . . If you have to listen to such stories, at least keep them to yourself. Look, look out of the window, girls. There are our grain carts, setting off to town. One after the other, cart after cart!

They all crowd in front of the windows to see the line of carts skirting the park. PROKHOR *crosses himself.*

PROKHOR

The eyes of all wait upon Thee, O Lord. They're off to town, to the market. To be sold. Five have gone, and there are more to come. Grain and timber – that's all that keeps us going. May they all get safely to the market. May Kostyga not get his hands on them . . .

MISHKA

Is it true, Uncle Prokhor, that Kostyga's men live under the ground, the whole lot of them, and that they even keep the smoke from their stoves hidden? And is it true that, long-long ago, five brothers lived here, and they quarrelled about how to share the land – always at each other's throats they were – and ever since then, this place has been called Pyatibratskoye, the Place of the Five Brothers? And that they strangled the rightful heir when he was still an infant, and made out he was a monster, and sent a newborn calf, bottled in spirits, to the Freak Museum in Petersburg? Here are more carts turning out of the gate into the road . . .

PROKHOR

Nine, ten, eleven. Oh Lord, Thou openest Thy hand and fillest all things. Twelve carts! Corn and timber, I tell you, that's all that keeps us going. Everything else is mortgaged. It may be that not even the grain is ours and the creditors are taking it away. We're not likely to be told! Of course it must have been him, the scatterbrain, rummaging about in the drawers, don't you think, Lusha? He's got sense enough to find a key that fits, but when it came to shutting the drawer and locking it, his lordship wouldn't think of that! Never has time for anything, always in a hurry, always in a rush! Nothing but wind in his head! . . There go two more carts. That seems to be the lot. Fourteen in all.

MISHKA

You were saying just now, Uncle Prokhor, that perhaps there's nothing left in Pyatibratskoye, everything has been mortgaged, perhaps even the corn belongs to the money-lenders. But what if that's really true? What if there's nothing left to sell in the estate, and the whole place is bare? What would happen then? What would become of the master and mistress? And of us, the servants?

PROKHOR

It would be very bad for us, my boy. All of us serfs would be sold at auction. The house servants one by one, and the peasants by whole villages. And that's only at the best – if we were not already mortgaged to some credit bank. For all I know, you and I may have belonged to strangers for a long time past. As though they'd tell us!

LUSHA

You can say what you like, that's a thing I'll never understand, not as long as I live. And yet nothing ought to surprise me, I ought to be used to everything by now. But even though I'm a slave myself, and my husband is a conscript, and my father and mother and all my family are slaves, I still can't get it into my head – how can I have been turned from a human being into a thing? I was dusting that cabinet just now, and I was afraid of scratching it. But who am I to be dusting that cabinet if I'm nothing but another piece of furniture belonging to the Count? Perhaps I'm not even worth as much as that cabinet. Perhaps I'm worth nothing at all. Who's to tell?

PROKHOR

Let me tell you, Lusha, you're certainly worth less than that cabinet. It's English marquetry, inlaid rosewood, made by Sheraton. It would cost as much as for four or five women like you. But don't rack your brains over that, my girl. Or you'll go out of your mind. How does it look now, Mishka? I haven't pulled it too far over?

MISHKA

Can't you see for yourself it's crooked? You might have hung it with your eyes shut!

PROKHOR

Yes, I know it's crooked. But it can't be helped. The window frame is out of true. There's a brick sticking out.

MISHKA

That must be the hole in the wall where the Countess, Domna the Murderess, had the cook bricked up alive?

PROKHOR

Mind what you say, boy. Still, there's no denying that she was more of a wild beast than a woman. They say she did away with near upon a hundred and fifty peasants – tortured them to death. And she liked to scare women and little children out of their wits. There's that fancy dress of hers – it's enough to make your flesh creep. It's still hanging in one of the cupboards. You've seen it, I dare say.

SIDOR

No, I haven't come across it.

LUSHA

I've neither seen nor heard of it.

MISHKA

Nor I.

GLASHA

I haven't either.
> *On the misty window panes, between the curtains, the gigantic shadows of two heads appear one after the other. Each in turn peers in from the garden.*

LUSHA

Oo, what a frightful thing!

PROKHOR

What's the matter?

LUSHA

Look at the window! No, not that one! The second from the left!

PROKHOR

Well, what about it?

LUSHA

Don't you see anything?

PROKHOR

What are you talking about? There's nothing there.

SIDOR

She's seeing things.

GLASHA

I saw it too.

LUSHA

A great giant in the garden – he stood on tiptoe and peeped through the window.

MISHKA

You dreamt it.

PROKHOR

Giant or no giant, now you've finished with the parquet, Sidor, you might take a duster and give the women a hand instead of standing around gaping.

SIDOR

Right you are, Prokhor Denisovich, I was going to do just that.

GLASHA

What was that fancy dress you were talking about? The one that belonged to that terrible great-grandmother of the Count's?

PROKHOR

Well, it looks as if we've nearly finished. I've just got one window left, and the curtains over the door. And you have only to dust the ornaments. As for the fancy dress, whenever the Count had visitors – when there was a ball, say, or a reception, or a banquet for the gentlemen and their ladies – a door would open and in she'd burst, like a bogyman, in a long black cloak, and a mask painted to look like a fish's head with whiskers and goggling eyes. She'd throw her arms out as if to grab hold of somebody – she'd turn right, then left, and they'd all be rolling on the floor or falling down in a dead faint like so many sheaves of corn. It's still there in the cupboard, that fine costume of hers. I'll go and have a look – if I find it I'll show you.

Exit. Once again, someone peers in at the window.

GLASHA

It's peeping in again! What d'you say now? We must look outside, open the window!

MISHKA

It's only the wind knocking a branch against the window pane, and the tree shutting out the light.

SIDOR

There's no wind outside, and no tree out there that I can remember. But let's have a look.

Opens the window.

You must have dreamed it. There's not a soul around. Now enough of all this talk, let's get down to work. Prokhor Denisovich is quite right. I'll help you with the dusting.

MISHKA

That fiend of a countess, she must have thought she could do whatever she liked. What did she care what anybody said, when she owned them all, body and soul? Yet she got her deserts in the end.

SIDOR

She wouldn't give up her lover to the Tsarina, that's how she got her deserts.

GLASHA

Sidor Pafnutyich, what a word to use! And in front of an innocent boy.

MISHKA

I'm not a child, Aunt Glasha. That's not a bad word. I don't know a more proper word than that.

SIDOR

She wouldn't give up her lover to the Empress Catherine, so they put a stop to her goings-on. As for the peasants she'd done to death, nobody worried about them – any more than about last year's snow.

A dog barks off-stage. SIDOR *goes to the window.*
Back, Khort, back. I won't let you in or you'll leave dirty marks on my parquet floor.

MISHKA

Is it true what I heard, that first they took away her title, and then they sentenced her to be hanged, but in the end they had mercy on her and let her live? And they say that when the hangman was flogging her on a high scaffold in the public square, a great crowd gathered round, and some even fainted, it was such a horrible sight. They poured water over them to bring them round. And some kind-hearted people threw paper money on to the scaffold, to bribe the hangman, so that he shouldn't be so hard on her.

Oh! Oh! Look what a fearful thing!

PROKHOR *runs in, wearing the fancy dress, with its painted catfish mask, of the legendary Domna the Murderess, and waves his arms as he had described her doing.* GLASHA *shrieks,* LUSHA *leans half fainting against the cupboard. Meanwhile,* SIDOR *climbs on to a chair and takes down the plaster head from the top of the cupboard, meaning to dust it. Seeing this,* PROKHOR *snatches off his mask and throws open his domino costume.*

PROKHOR

(*shouts*): Now, now, you fathead! Take your hands off that thing. Put it down at once before you break it.

SIDOR

Instead of telling me what to do, Prokhor Denisovich, you'd better get some sense into your own head and not go scaring women with that painted mug when they are with child. They could easily have a miscarriage, or give birth to a monster. As to that head, it's like any other head, and nothing is going to happen to it. You don't need to tell me. It's the head of that young rascal on whose account Domna fell out with the Empress, I know all about it . . . And if it isn't him . . .

PROKHOR *takes off the domino and absentmindedly leaves it with the mask on an armchair at the far end of the room.*

PROKHOR

What are you mauling it like that for, you wretched sinner? All right, you've dusted it, now put it back.

SIDOR

And if it's not that harum-scarum, I still know whose graven image it is. It's that boy that Domna gave birth to, when she was being kept on a chain in a convent cell – she had him by one of the guards. People say he was taken back to the estate, and brought up here in secret. They made him a guards officer when he grew up, so people say. That's his head all right. But what became of him in the end, nobody knows.

MISHKA

Good, Uncle Prokhor! You've finished that last window and put the curtain up over the door as well, and I never even saw you doing it. Only you've hung it crooked, the fringe on the left is trailing on the floor. Bunch it up nicely into the cornice. And now draw the cord and let the folds fan out. Is it true what they say, that his lordship's valet, Platon Shcheglov, is sweet on our mistress and is always standing up for her. In plain Russian – he's her fancy man.

PROKHOR

Where do you pick up such words, you snotty little scamp? Look at what you've done to Aunt Lusha, you've made her blush for shame.

LUSHA

Shame indeed! What next? Why should I be ashamed? It's just that I don't feel well. My throat hurts and I can hardly breathe.

SIDOR

Come, come Lusha, you can't get out of it like that. As soon as you heard Platon's name, you blushed as red as a poppy.

c

LUSHA

How can you say such things? Poppy indeed! I'm a married woman. What do I care about your Platon? A fine treasure you've found.

PROKHOR

But you could never take your eyes off him.

LUSHA

So what if I couldn't? It's easy to make a girl's heart flutter.

SIDOR

(*in a strangled voice*): We're done for! They're coming!

PROKHOR

So they are. The village children are scampering off the road as if they'd seen a bear. I can see the horses . . . and there's the coach.
At the first mention of her master and mistress, LUSHA *falls down in a dead faint. The others, too, are terrified and rush about in confusion.*

SIDOR

They'll be here at once!

PROKHOR

Quick, Mishka, run to the servants' hall, get everyone to come and sing a welcome for the master and mistress!
Exit Mishka.
What are you all dashing about for like madmen? Can't you see the coach has halted in front of the estate office? Look, the manager has stopped it to give us time to finish our work. But

we're ready anyway, all the rooms are as tidy as can be. Goodness! Look at Lusha sprawling on the floor! What a to-do!

SIDOR

She's picked a fine time to faint! Any minute they'll come in and see her – that won't do at all.

PROKHOR

What's the matter with her? Some woman's ailment, d'you think?

GLASHA

She's with child.

PROKHOR

So are you.

GLASHA

I'm stronger than she is.

PROKHOR

Don't be a fool! She's no more ill than I am! She just heard us say 'they're coming', that's what made her faint. Which of us does not tremble and feel faint when the master's eye is upon him?

SIDOR

Even just to hear their voices, I go numb all over.

GLASHA

It makes me tremble like a leaf. My blood runs cold. Lusha, Lusha darling, drink a little water! Here, I'll sprinkle some over you. Come on, you silly, wake up! This is not the time to faint.

SIDOR

We must lift her up and carry her out. Next thing they'll drive up, and when they come in and see her they'll be cross.

GLASHA

Get up, get up, Lusha. The master is coming. Pull your dress down, tidy yourself up.

LUSHA *gets up, pulls down her dress and draws her hand over her eyes and forehead.*

PROKHOR

You were telling me not to frighten women with that painted mask when they're in the family way. But what's a painted mask to you if you live a serf's life? Yet our master and mistress aren't like others, they're kindness itself. You won't find their likes anywhere. And yet it's enough for a girl to hear someone say 'the master is coming' for her to drop down in a dead faint. That's how frightened they are of their masters, the peasants of Russia.

LUSHA

I don't know what came over me. My heart seemed to stop from foreboding.

Enter an outrider, the footman FEDOSEY DULYCH, *wearing a braided cloak, and carrying two heavy suitcases, which he puts down on a plain wooden bench by the door.*

DULYCH

Well, here we are, like a bolt from the blue. I bet you missed us. You must be worn out with waiting.

PROKHOR

We're all right, thanks be to God. Nothing to complain of.

DULYCH

Put all the travelling things here, when they bring them in from the coach. Get the water ready for the mistress in her dressing room. And get the steam up in the bathhouse for his lordship. Supper for two in the morning room. Why haven't you lit the lamps yet? Look how dark it is.

PROKHOR

It seems dark to you because you've come in from outside. It's early yet. They'd say we're wasting the master's oil.

DULYCH

Mishka nearly knocked me over, rushing down the stairs. Where was he off to?

PROKHOR

We wanted to greet the master and mistress properly – with a song of welcome.

DULYCH

There's no need for that, no need at all. They've got other things to think about. They've been quarrelling all the way. She's been crying her eyes out. And he's in a devil of a temper.

PROKHOR

Why's that? What's the trouble?

DULYCH

Only the usual business. Lawsuits. And no money. How is he to save himself from ruin? I can't tell you what a journey we've had, God help us! He kept on and on at her about the diamonds. Give them to me, he said, give them to me. A little more and they'd have come to blows. Then Platon, the clever boy, put his nose in – the Count nearly killed him. Hush. . . . They're coming. It's them.

> *He steps aside to make way for those who are coming in. He and the servants, who are now huddled together at the far end of the study, expect the Count and Countess to appear, but instead,* PLATON SHCHEGLOV *walks in, silent and thoughtful, carrying a lot of small bags and hold-alls, which he puts down beside the suitcases after greeting the servants with a nod. He is followed a moment later by the Countess,* ELENA ARTE-MYEVNA, *in a long travelling cloak, her veil low over her face. Unused to the darkness in the room, she takes a few uncertain steps and pauses near the door. The servants, crowded at the back of the room, wait in silence for their mistress to take notice of them, but she either doesn't see them or is in no hurry to do so.*

ELENA

Here already, Max? I didn't see you pass me. Please not now, we'll talk about it later. (*Realises her mistake.*) Again I've mistaken you for the master, Platon.

PLATON

God knows what will become of me. If only my mind could be at peace about you. Won't you give in to him, your ladyship? If not, he'll plague the life out of you over those jewels.

ELENA

Oh, for goodness' sake, Platon! Give him the jewels? Not for anything in the world! They're beyond all price. I'd sooner give them secretly to you, slip them into your hand, in some dark corner, so that you can run away somewhere, far beyond the Danube. He'll make life unbearable for you here. He'll never forgive you for that piece of impudence.

PLATON

Give in to him, my lady. And stop all this wild talk. You're ruining your life. And remember, I'm not made of wood or stone.

ELENA

Wait. Be quiet. I didn't see them. They're looking at us. All right now, they've turned away. Listen to me. We can't hide from God – He sees us. But we are innocent before him. We have committed no sin, yet.

He stares at her in astonishment. In reply she bursts into happy, feminine laughter.

That wasn't sin yet, you silly! Wait a moment, they're staring at us again, damn them. All right. They're looking away. I'll tell you what we'll do, you and I. We'll have a child, a cherub, a pretty madcap of a boy – the kind that act in plays. That will be a sin all right! And yet, I don't know that it will be, even then. To hell with them! I'll teach them to stare, the brazen creatures. Wait, I'll call Prokhor and tell him to send them away. Prokhor! Come here, Prokhor! Ah, how do you do, Prokhor? How are things with you?

PROKHOR *comes nearer.*

PROKHOR

Thank you, your ladyship, welcome home! I hope you are in good health. I'm sorry, your ladyship, please forgive me, don't be angry with me, but you should, perhaps, say how–do–you–do to the servants. They're devoted to you heart and soul, they've been watching you, waiting for a sign, but you haven't given them a glance, it makes them sad. Please forgive me for speaking frankly. I mean it well.

ELENA

Why should I be angry with you? On the contrary, thank you for telling me. I was just going to talk to them and say something nice. But meanwhile, this is what I want you to do, Prokhor. I have no secrets from you. I'm not afraid of you. I need to talk something over with Platon in private. You know he's my one support. He came to me with my dowry. He's one of my own people, from Sumtsovo, he belonged to my father.

Getting more and more worked up she speaks in a loud, angry voice.

All of you in Pyatibratskoye, you'd like to strip me bare, to take all I have, to make a beggar of me. But I won't let myself be eaten up alive! You won't get your way!

PROKHOR

Your ladyship! your ladyship!

ELENA

(*controlling herself*): Oh Lord, I didn't mean to lose my temper. I'm sorry, I feel so ashamed! I can hardly get my breath. As I was saying to you, Prokhor, Platon is my one support, the only one who stands up for me, the only one who pities me in my troubles. I must talk to him alone. I'll send the servants away myself. Meanwhile you go down. The manager is pestering the master with all his tales. You talk to him as well. About the coach springs having to be repaired, and the horses needing this and that. Go, my dear, and keep him talking as long as you can. You see how I trust you. I'm not afraid of you!

PROKHOR

Oh, my lady! What can I say? I can't help but warn you. You're not on the right road. Please don't judge me for speaking up as I think. As for you, Platon, there's nothing to be said: you know what you're doing and you will answer for it. You're putting your neck into the noose of your own free will. I'll go and do as your ladyship says. Only I must warn you, if you want to be alone: the servants are getting ready to welcome you. It's this room they'll come to, the whole crowd of them, with the bread and salt.

ELENA

That really has no sense! There's no need for that at all. As you go down to the coach-house, look into the servants' hall and tell them I forbid it. The last thing we want is to have them all bursting in! Go along, my dear friend.

PROKHOR

I will, your ladyship. (*Exit.*)
Elena goes up to the group of servants at the back of the room. The floor-polisher and the chamber maids bow from the waist, press their lips to her outstretched hand and kiss her on the shoulder.

ELENA

How are you, my dear ones. Thank you for your welcome, for your devotion, for your faithful service. How are you all?

SIDOR

Thanks, to your kind prayers, our lady, we are safe and sound. How can we come to harm when you shelter us like a wall.

ELENA

I know we've arrived at an untimely moment, when you were not expecting us.

LUSHA

It's an honour, we are all the happier for that.

ELENA

We've come like a bolt from the blue . . .

GLASHA

Heavens above, no! Not at all!

ELENA

But we didn't mean to catch you unawares. We didn't do
it on purpose. It was just that his lordship was suddenly so
anxious to get home. We managed to save two days on the
journey, but the men are tired out and the horses at their last
gasp.

LUSHA

Don't you worry about that, my lady. They'll be as right as
rain when they've had a rest.

ELENA

Can you tell me, Sidor, why it is that all along the boundaries
of the estate, both at Sumtsovo and here, we kept meeting
strangers? From the coach I couldn't make out who they were.
One used to come across them before – wayfarers, pilgrims,
crippled beggars, but nothing like so many as now. This time
they seemed to be everywhere, walking along and not even
bothering to look at us. Vagrants of some sort . . .

LUSHA

That's just what they are, my lady.

SIDOR

There's been a lot of trouble and disorder in the military settlements.

ELENA

There was a mutiny, I heard, is that true?

SIDOR

Yes, it is, your ladyship.

ELENA

That's very sad, and the consequences will be sadder still.

SIDOR

You've never heard of such goings on. And when it came to the inquiry and to punishing the guilty, the ringleaders vanished into thin air – and so did the others they'd dragged into it against their will.

GLASHA

That's why the woods are full of homeless riff-raff.

LUSHA

And the highwaymen are on the move as well. They're getting bolder. They even creep up to the kitchen doors, they aren't afraid of anything.

SIDOR

And the conscripts are getting out of hand – when they were being taken away they boasted that they'd soon be back home again!

ELENA

(*crosses herself*): Saints in Heaven, what horrors everywhere!

May God save us from such things. It's like a nightmare, but the Lord is merciful. And now, I'll tell you what, my dear people: I'm tired out from the journey. Go along now, you have my permission. I want to be alone.

SIDOR

Yes, we are going now, may it please your ladyship. But I beg leave to tell you that the village people are getting ready to give you a welcome.

ELENA

I know. I sent word to tell them not to. Will you make sure, as you go down? Say I asked for it to be called off.

SIDOR

Yes, my lady.

LUSHA

We'll go and tell them.

GLASHA

Just as you wish, my lady.
    Exit.

ELENA

At last! I thought we'd never be rid of them! Quick now, Platon. Don't stand there like a post. Every second is precious. Any moment the master will come in and start pestering me about those jewels. I won't give in to him at any price. Not as long as I live. But what can I say to get rid of him? And fancy that wretched Prokhor giving me a piece of his mind like that! 'You're not on the right road!' I'll show him the right road! I'll teach him, the fool! Well, why don't you say something!

PLATON

Tell him you can't remember where you put them: you've looked everywhere and couldn't find them. But it would be better to give them up.

ELENA

That's no good! He'll never believe me. He'll only laugh in my face and tell me to stop play-acting! Even the maids know where they are. All my jewels are in their cases, locked up in my writing desk. Can't you think of anything better?

PLATON

Say they were there, but they aren't there now! They've disappeared.

ELENA

He'd set the whole neighbourhood by the ears. Straton Nalyotov and his soldiers would be all over the place. They'd turn everything upside down, and flog everybody, trying to find the stolen goods.

PLATON

If only we could gain a week's time!

ELENA

Why a week? What are you hoping for?

PLATON

I don't really know myself. But there's something in the air. Something will happen soon.

ELENA

Why a week? That Prokhor – there's someone I'd like to see

beaten by the soldiers. But why do you say a week? Quiet. Hush. Here's the master!

> *Enter* COUNT MAX, *lean, arrogant, wilful, about forty, clean-shaven; a nervous tic affects his face and shoulder and he has a deep scar along the left cheek, from an operation or a wound. He carries a case of duelling pistols.*

MAX

I hope I'm not intruding?

ELENA

What rubbish! Why this play-acting?

MAX

Will you take the pistols, Platon. One of them keeps jamming. Unload them both, and oil them. You won't injure yourself?

PLATON

You must be joking, my lord. I've cleaned them for you time and again. And it was me you sent to Petersburg to buy them after you had seen them advertised. You must have forgotten.

MAX

Quiet! Don't argue! How they all let their tongues run away with them. Stick to the point, like a soldier.

PLATON

Yes, sir.

MAX

That's better. Now get out. I'll deal with you later.

PLATON

As you wish, my lord.
> *Exit with the pistol case.*

MAX

At last we're alone, without strangers. And at home. How I've longed for this moment! What a joy! And I have so many plans, so many ideas for the future. If you only knew what's going on in my head! I can see it all so clearly!

ELENA

I am very glad.

MAX

I am determined, now, without delay, without wasting time over the preparations, to lay the foundations of a completely new way of life. You'll give me your precious playthings now. I'll take them to town tomorrow, to be valued – they'll give me credit again, and everything will run like clockwork from then on.

ELENA

But you are still in your travelling boots and cloak. And I'm dead tired from the journey, and I haven't had time to change. Better sleep on it, Max. Leave it until tomorrow.

MAX

I can't go on like this. We are on the verge of ruin. But it's not too late: Christian Frantsevich says that with a few really decisive measures . . .

ELENA

Tomorrow, Max.

MAX

I come back to my estate and it's as though the whole place were bewitched. Everything is confused. It's impossible to understand anything. You daren't punish a servant for fear he might be a relation – a cousin or an uncle! Who is that handsome fellow on top of the cupboard, I ask you, whom all of us here so mysteriously resemble? Is he the founder of our noble line or the forefather of our serfs? How far does my authority extend, and where do the highwaymen of Prince's Wood take over? But that's not the point. The point is that our traditional farming methods are out of date and not of the slightest use nowadays.

ELENA

That's enough! It's too much. I know everything you are going to say.

MAX

Why are you shouting?

ELENA

And why are you always talking so grandly, and telling lies, and making promises you don't mean to keep? Now you're going to free the peasants – but only in words, of course – and let them pay a tax instead of working on your fields. You'll free the house serfs too, but it's all words. I've heard it all over and over again. I've had enough! Enough!

MAX

Do you really think I don't mean it?

ELENA

You mean it, do you? Then why all the talk?

*She starts up from her arm-chair, without noticing that she
had been sitting on the fancy dress. In extreme irritation, runs
up to one of the tables.*

Here you are. Here's a nice sharp pen. And here's ink and
paper. Kindly sit down and write a declaration emancipating
all the serfs. I'll tell you what to say, if you don't know. In the
village of Pyatibratskoye, this twentieth day of October
eighteen hundred and thirty-five. It's the feast of Saint Artemis
the Martyr – my father's namesday, and I'd quite forgotten,
bad daughter that I am. Well, why aren't you writing? What
are you waiting for? So it's nothing but high-sounding words,
as usual! They aren't worth much, your good intentions.

*She goes back to her arm-chair and notices the domino and the
mask flung over the back.*

What's that?

MAX

Show me, let me look. That's the carnival dress that belonged
to my great-grandmother, Countess Domna. How on earth
did it get into my study? It's disgraceful. Who dared ...

ELENA

The servants were tidying the house, carrying things from one
room to another. It was an oversight. And supposing even
that they did amuse themselves while we were away, must we
start by punishing them? It was only carelessness. But don't
try to change the subject by talking about Domna. What about
that deed of emancipation? As usual, you don't mean a word of
it.

MAX

I'll prove to you that you are wrong. This isn't something you
can do by a stroke of the pen. We must get in touch with the

D

district land authorities, and have a proper document drawn up. They're sure to raise difficulties at the District Court. I know exactly what they'll say. But this is just where I need your help: we can overcome all these obstacles. Where are your diamonds?

ELENA

This is utterly inhuman. Why can't we leave it until tomorrow?

MAX

Who are you keeping these treasures for? We have no children.

ELENA

Are you throwing that in *my* face?

MAX

Oh, no. It's my fault, I know. I'm an old rake. But that doesn't change the fact that when we die, Pyatibratskoye, which by then will be in a flourishing condition owing to my improvements, will go to my nephew, Count Iriney. As you know perfectly well.

ELENA

A fine and very promising young man. You can't hold a candle to him.

MAX

Funny tastes he has, I must say. Theatres, writers, and all that kind of nonsense.

ELENA

I suppose it's better to squander hundreds of thousands, spending your time with your cronies in taverns and brothels.

MAX

Are you quite determined to make me lose my temper? How can I get it into your head that it's your own interests you're damaging by your obstinacy? You don't understand a thing – when it comes to practical matters you're a perfect idiot. It's to your own advantage to entrust those jewels to me for a couple of days. Come on, give me those jewel cases. You're driving me out of my mind.

ELENA

I'm too tired.

MAX

Come on, now – they're not paving stones. I'll fetch them myself if you tell me where they are.

ELENA

But that's just the trouble: I simply can't remember where I put them last time. I had them in my hands just before we left, I was putting them somewhere but there were so many things to distract me. The horses were waiting. And you were telling me to hurry. I don't even know where to look for them now. My mind is a complete blank. Tomorrow I'll get up early and it will all gradually come back to me. Be patient.

MAX

Well, if it's only that, I think I can help you. I have a fairly good idea where these brooches and necklaces and things are kept. I'll go and get them.
Walks quickly out of the room.

ELENA

Max! Max! Don't do that. Come back! I'll find them myself.

Runs out of the room after him. For a while the stage is empty. Outside it begins to snow, then gradually stops. Once again, the shadows of two heads appear, one after the other. Then the window opens quietly and through it, silently and cautiously, KOSTYGA *and* LYOSHKA LESHAKOV *climb in.* KOSTYGA *makes straight for the arm-chair and, looking over his shoulder, ears strained for every sound, starts trying on Domna's fancy dress.*

KOSTYGA

Their servant was trying it on.

LYOSHKA

That was the butler, Prokhor. I saw him.

KOSTYGA

Let's take it.

LYOSHKA

What good is it?

KOSTYGA

It's too dark to tell. We'll find a use for it later.

LYOSHKA

(*looking round him*): This is where I used to bring bundles of firewood and light the stove. There's a flue up here, a length of pipe.

KOSTYGA

(*wearing the domino and the mask, and about to take them off*): A stove pipe?

LYOSHKA

That's right, a stove pipe.

KOSTYGA

What's it like, tell me quickly.

LYOSHKA

Let's run for it. Someone's coming.

LYOSHKA *climbs out of the window and pulls it shut.* KOS-
TYGA, *who has not had time to take off the domino and the
mask, hides behind the cupboard.* ELENA, *in tears and biting
her lips, runs into the room. The snow has been falling on and
off, but has now quite stopped. In the rifts between the scudding
clouds, the full moon shines brightly. Elena thinks aloud,
walking excitedly up and down in front of the window, and
every time the moon shows between the clouds, she turns
unconsciously towards it, as though drawn by it, and as though
by this gesture turning from the dark depths of her heart to the
brightness in the sky.*

ELENA

To accuse me of being a commoner on top of everything
else! 'We Norovtsevs go back to Rurik, while you Sumtsovs
were ennobled only the other day.' Why have I come back
here and left him all alone in my room? I thought I heard
voices. I thought it must be Platon talking to someone. God,
how desperately I need him now. Just for a moment, just to
have a word with him. Meanwhile that insufferable lout is on
the rampage, breaking into my desk and turning everything
upside down. I'll show you whether the Sumtsovs are com-
moners! My dowry wasn't too common for you, was it?
Thief, thief! And it's for this rake-hell that I gave up everything, my innocence, my friends, my happiness in my father's
house. There was a fancy dress lying on the arm-chair. Where
can it have got to? Such mad things happening all the time,
such unfathomable mysteries at every step. So the Sumtsovs

are not nobles, but bullying people and ransacking their things – that's noble, I suppose! Poor Gideon, how he's gone downhill, after all the hopes we had of him! First to study for the priesthood and then to end up as a mechanic! All the same I've fooled you, you Rurik with a crowbar. A lot of the jewels are on me, in the little bag inside my belt. I wish it were all of them, but I had only time to take less than half. I was getting them out of the desk in a hurry before we left. I put buckshot into the empty cases to make them heavy. But they were calling me to get into the coach. I had to go before I'd finished. What do I care for all this luxury, it can go to the devil! I'd like to throw all these cases and caskets at him, straight into his greedy face! Take them and may they choke you. If it weren't for Platon. For his sake I mustn't let go of these what d'you call them, (*laughs*) these so-called reins of power! Even as a child I couldn't bear that he should be a serf. How ill it suits him to be a lackey, to obey and flatter, to bow and scrape. It's so unlike him! They say there's a mystery about his birth. But what do I care! What do I care, Platon? The moment we have waited for so long has come. Your slavery is at an end. We've had enough. I'll free you this very day. I don't yet know how, but I know I'll do it. You'll be able to raise your head at last. You'll be free, you'll fly far away from me, my falcon! And later on, who knows, perhaps I'll follow you. Who knows what may happen here!

Wildly happy, she jumps from chair to chair, then pulls herself together and starts, as though coming out of a trance.

But I must hurry back to my room. Goodness knows what that lout will do next. (*Exit.*)

LYOSHKA's *head appears at the window and disappears again. A moment later,* COUNT MAX *walks hurriedly into the room, jewel cases sticking out of his pockets; he has several in his arms and is hugging others to his chest. Loaded with them to the chin he is hampered in his movements and his speech.* ELENA *runs in after him, trying to snatch the cases back and shouting.*

ELENA

Don't you dare! They're mine. Give them back to me! I told you I'd give them to you myself, but not now.

MAX

A likely story! I'll get them back, will I, after my valet and your lover has run off with them! Did you think I didn't know? Well, you were mistaken. I know everything. It's all out.

ELENA

How vile you are! I know who's behind this. It's the Surepyevs' doing. And you believe their wicked lies, and have no idea why they hate me so. Their daughter, Lusha, is head over heels in love with Shcheglov, she's out of her mind about him, so she sees what isn't there.

MAX

That's because she's jealous of you.

ELENA

What a disgusting lie! Admit this minute that you are wrong! You will apologise to me at once.
> *She runs up to him and snatches the jewel cases from his hands. He lets several of them fall and can't bend down to pick them up, hampered as he is by the others.*

Slanderer! Thief! Give them back to me, every one of them!
> *With his free hand,* COUNT MAX *pushes her away so violently that she falls to the ground.*

Help! Help!

PLATON SHCHEGLOV *bursts into the room, carrying the pistol case which he flings down on a table. He hurries across to the* COUNTESS *to help her get up. She half hides behind a tall arm-chair, in case the* COUNT *should attack her again. At the same time* PLATON *bars the* COUNT'S *way, grips his arms and, pulling them up by the wrists, holds them tightly. Everything* MAX *had been holding falls to the ground. Absorbed in these extraordinary happenings, the two protagonists pay no attention to the objects scattered on the floor. Only later will these priceless riches attract attention, leading some into temptation and recalling others to conscience and duty.*

PLATON

(*recklessly*): Don't lay a finger on her ladyship, my lord! I won't allow a hair of her head to be harmed. I'd go through fire for her.

MAX

(*furiously twisting this way and that, trying unsuccessfully to break* PLATON'S *grip*): What! So you dare to raise your hand against the master God has given you! You'll pay for this with your life, blackguard! It's not enough for you to do these terrible things you have the insolence to shout about them for all the world to hear! Well, don't expect any mercy from me! They'll break every bone in your body, down in the stables!

ELENA

Don't believe him! Don't be afraid! Don't let him go, Platon. I'll lie across the doorway, I'll cling to their knees, I won't let them!

PLATON

(*struck by a sudden thought and as though inspired*): Don't struggle,

my lord! I'll let you go. I know I'm finished! I've staked my
life, and there's no way back for me now. Here are the pistols.
I've not unloaded either of them. As soon as I free your hands,
take one and shoot. They taught you to shoot in the guards,
you won't miss. But since nothing is ever certain – man hopes
for one thing and then God wills another, so give me your
word as a nobleman, as a Count, that, should I escape death,
the next shot will be mine, and you will stand and wait
for me to fire.

MAX

It's the end of the world! It's beyond all reason: either I'm
mad or the whole world has gone out of its mind. A shoe-black,
a scullion, challenging me to a duel! And my faithful consort
acting as his second! A charming scene! But you won't get
your way. I shall call my loyal servants. They'll tie you up and
take you to the town. And there you will be hanged without
so much as a trial for assaulting your master. As for you. . . .
you . . .

ELENA

Well?

MAX

I'll write to your aunt, the Abbess Fedulia, and ask her to take
you into her convent: she'll see to it that you mend your ways.
Enter PROKHOR; *in his haste he doesn't notice what is
happening, or the state the* COUNTESS *is in, and addresses
her.*

PROKHOR

Forgive me for presuming to come in without permission.
It's about the singers. I came to warn you that they won't

listen to me, it's like talking to a brick wall. I told them, you didn't want them crowding into the house. But they go on saying that the whole village has been ordered out, to come and sing a song of welcome. They'll be bursting in any minute.

Only now notices what has been happening between PLATON *and the* COUNT.

Oh God! Oh God! What is this? Are you out of your mind, Platon? Raising your hand against your master! Stop this outrage at once. Throw yourself at his lordship's feet and beg him to forgive you and to spare your life. Say the devil led you astray. Your ladyship, our mistress, our mother, tell him to come to his senses. He'll listen to you.

ELENA

Well done, Platon, splendid! Be reckless, crazy, desperate! Stake everything on one throw. Fight him, it's a wonderful idea. Shoot, Max. He's doing you an honour. Or I'll take his place, if you think it's below your dignity.

PROKHOR

Lord, have mercy on us. . . . Would that my ears had not heard nor my eyes seen . . .

He tries to drag PLATON *away from the* COUNT, *but* ELENA *holds on to him, and* PROKHOR *is helpless because he dare not touch her.*

MAX

Why don't you use your hands, Prokhor? You daren't touch her? You can do what you like to her. Slap her face, the lying bitch, the deceitful whore. The viper I've nurtured. I disown her. She is not your mistress any longer. Kill her, and I'll reward you with your freedom! What's that commotion down below?

PROKHOR

(*buries his head in his hands*): Oh God! Everything is falling apart. There's nothing but trouble. Those are the villagers, my lord – they know nothing, they're coming with the bread and salt to sing you their welcome. I'll run down and tell them to go.

MAX

Don't do that. Tell them to come in. Say the Count will be happy to see them. They are faithful servants, they'll take my side.

The room begins to fill with peasants and servants, come to welcome their master home. Ahead of all the rest comes MISHKA, *carrying a small icon on an embroidered cloth over his shoulder; then* FROL DRYAGIN, *carrying the tray with the bread and salt. When they take in the extraordinary scene, the peasants, men and women, exchange bewildered glances, shuffle their feet and crowd together near the door. The icon is carried away, the tray with the bread and salt disappears. The crowd begins to disperse.* PAKHOM SUREPYEV, LUSHA'S *father, comes forward, bends down and, staring hypnotised at the jewel cases scattered on the floor, starts picking them up. Glancing furtively at the watching crowd, he takes the cases to the back of the room and puts them on a table, trying by his whole bearing to convey that he is doing this to safeguard the master's property.*

PAKHOM

(*shakes his head*): Lord! What a to-do! We're all at sixes and sevens!

PROKHOR

Pakhom, you can see they've both gone out of their minds. Come and help me part them.

PAKHOM *and* PROKHOR *try to separate the* COUNT *and* SHCHEGLOV, *but once again the* COUNTESS *prevents them.*

PROKHOR

Don't, my lady. You don't know what you're doing. For shame! Come to your senses. And you're a fine one, Pakhom – picking up other people's jewel boxes! Do you think I didn't see you? You'd better watch out! Look how fast they're holding on to one another. There's no dragging them apart. Take your hands away, my lady.

At that moment the COUNT *manages to break loose, runs over to the pistol-case, seizes one of the pistols and, after making sure that it is loaded, aims it at* PLATON *who has had time to move away and is standing with his back against the cupboard door. The* COUNT *takes long and careful aim, but because he is tired out, and upset by his ordeal, his arm jerks with increasing violence; he grits his teeth, trying to control the spasm and waiting for it to end. Through the dwindling crowd of servants,* LUSHA *runs in from the back of the house and stands in front of* PLATON, *shielding him with her body.*

LUSHA

(*falling on her knees*): Don't harm him, my lord. Even though he's forfeited his life, spare him, have mercy on him. I dare not say whose fault it was, but he is not to blame. Let me answer for him, punish me instead if somebody must be punished.

A shot rings out. The bullet strikes the plaster head on top of the cupboard and smashes it into large and small fragments; a cloud of white dust envelops those who are standing near.

MAX

Oh hell! That wretched twitch spoilt my aim. I fired too high.

LUSHA

Oh Lord, Oh Lord, how it hurts! Help! I'm done for. It's burnt my eyes out, I can't see.

PAKHOM

It's the plaster dust that's got into them. Let me wipe it off for you.

LUSHA

No, don't, father, it makes it worse! It's as though they'd been slashed with a knife. I can't bear it! I'm done for! I can't see!

A Voice in the Crowd

No wonder you can't see in this dark! What we need is a light.

A lighted candle is brought in on a candle-stick.

PAKHOM

Come outside, Lusha. Let's wash your eyes.

MAX

Have I been such a harsh master to you that not one of you will stand up for me?

FROL

What are your orders, my lord? I'm at your service, heart and soul.

MAX

Listen, my good fellow.

FROL

Yes, my lord.

MAX

Saddle a horse, the fastest we have.

FROL

That's Thunderbolt.

MAX

I thought Eagle was. But whichever you think best.

FROL

Thunderbolt is our fastest stallion.

MAX

Saddle him then. And ride over as fast as you can to Straton Silantyevich. Tell him we need soldiers at Pyatibratskoye without delay. Say there's a rebellion on the estate. Do that, Frol, and I'll not forget your help. I'll make you a village elder.

FROL

I thank you humbly, my lord. I'll go this minute. And when I come back, I'll bring the soldiers with me.

PAKHOM

(*who has come up without anyone noticing him*): A dreadful thing has happened, sir. My daughter Lusha has gone blind, it seems. Tell Straton, Frol, that there's trouble on the estate. Say we are all at sixes and sevens. Everything is going from bad to worse. People have gone out of their minds and they're up to no good.

FROL

(*crossly*): Don't you try to teach me. I know what I have to say.

Voice from the Crowd

That's a fine thing, Frol! Selling out your own people, are you? You devil!

Murmur of discontent.

FROL

(*in a low voice*): What d'you know about it, you fool? Words don't always mean what they say.

Instead of hurrying to the stables to carry out his master's orders, he slips through the crowd at the back of the room and goes up to the table on which PLATON *has left the pistol case and* PROKHOR *the jewellery; stealthily he gathers the jewels in a pile on the edge of the table. The confusion grows. Strangers, wearing peasant coats and caps, slip into the room and mingle with the crowd. Someone opens now one window, now another, and leaves them wide. Beyond the trees of the park appear two or three small lights which move continually from side to side. The house seems less and less shut off from the country outside.* PROKHOR *makes super-human but vain efforts to defend its privacy.*

MAX

My faithful servants! Don't be led astray. Take no notice of all this bedlam, the shouting, the quarrelling, the shooting.

A few isolated Voices

We understand, Sir. It's the master's business. These things happen once in a while. They can't be helped.

MAX

A man has behaved outrageously. A woman has gone out of her mind. But nothing has happened that is past mending.

PROKHOR

Who's playing about with the windows? It's not summertime – letting cold air into heated rooms like that! Why are you groaning, Lusha my sweet? Are you still no better?

LUSHA

It hurts so much I can't bear it. I can't see a thing, Prokhor!

PROKHOR

Where has Platon got to? There's no sign of him. Ah, Platon, Platon, I told you often enough, but you wouldn't listen. Now look at all the trouble you have caused! And this is only the beginning, there's still worse to come!

LUSHA

Oh, I can't stand it! Oh, how it hurts! What have I done to deserve it? Am I really going to be blind?

MAX

All this unpleasantness will be looked into. The truth will come out. No one is going to get away with anything! Has Frol gone for Straton Silantyevich?

A dog barks off stage.

Isolated Voices

Back, Khort, back. You can't come in. Frol took the horse and galloped off. No, he didn't, he's been hanging around here. There he is over there. He never left at all. . . . You're lying, I saw him go out. And if he went out, it means he rode away. Go away, Khort. Get out!

Voices

Lyoshka Leshakov! Lyoshka Leshakov!

LUSHA

Oh, it's more than flesh and blood can stand! How can such a thing happen to me? What is to become of me, where shall I go, what shall I do without my sight?

Dog barks off stage.

Voices

Lyoshka Leshakov!

MAX

Leshakov! Where is he? Get hold of him, don't let him go.

Voices

There's no one here. The lies people tell! They're seeing things.

MAX

They're seeing things, all right! Enough of all this chatter, hold your tongues! When the soldiers come, I'll put you all in your place. If you're innocent, not a hair of your head will be harmed. You don't know what a happy future is in store for you. My estate has gone to rack and ruin, but we'll work together for a year or two and we'll build it up again. You'll work with your hands and I with my brains. And I'll never forget those of you who have helped me: I'll give every single one of you complete freedom. Do you understand?

LUSHA

I'm done for! I can't see anything! It's pitch dark all round.

Voices

Thank you, master, for your goodness. Thank you, kind master, thank you for your promises.

E

The peasants bow from the waist, then kneel down and touch the ground with their foreheads.

PROKHOR

Again somebody's fiddling with those windows. Stop it or I'll show you what for! Who are you anyway, where have you come from? I'm asking you, you vermin. Get out, clear off while the going's good, or I'll call the police! And where's the mistress? No sign of her. I didn't see her go and now she's vanished. Pray God she hasn't run off to the lake. Next thing she'll throw herself into it! Can't somebody run and see where she is? It's like talking to the deaf. They don't care. Nobody listens. Platon, Platon, you good-for-nothing, look what you've done, look at all the havoc you have caused.

PAKHOM

And why didn't you stop him? That's the last we'll see of him now. He's bolted, your Platon. He must have slipped out through the window long ago.

MAX

(*as if only now coming to*): Platon? Did you say Platon? Where is he? Stop him, tie him up! It's all his fault. And if he's bolted, go after him, all of you, and bring him back, dead or alive!

LUSHA

I'll never see the light of day again, and when my darling comes back from soldiering, what'll be the good of a blind wife to him?

PROKHOR

What a business, what a business! And nobody turns a hair. I'll run along and look for her ladyship myself, my lord. I'll go

and call her. I'm worried about her. And I'll go to the stables to
see if Frol has left.

MAX

Run along, my good fellow. And if Frol hasn't gone yet, take a
horse yourself and ride as fast as you can.

PROKHOR

Yes, my lord. I won't come back till I've seen to it.
    Exit. GLASHA *and* SIDOR *only now come running into the
    room, and* MISHKA *returns.*

GLASHA

Lusha, Lusha my treasure! Mishka says you've gone blind. I
can't believe it. How did it happen?

LUSHA

It was that accursed stone head. I'm finished, I'm done for. If
you love me, wish me a quick death.

SIDOR

Don't despair, Lusha. There's a candle on the table, can you
see it?

LUSHA

It's just a blur, like a will-o-the-wisp.

SIDOR

That's a ray of hope. It means that the doctor in the town will
be able to make you see again.

GLASHA

And they say Platon came to blows with the master, can it
be true? Who's ever heard of such a thing!

Wearing DOMNA'S *fancy dress,* KOSTYGA *jumps out from behind the cupboard and fools about, waving his arms and dashing this way and that at the far end of the room.*

MISHKA

Uncle Prokhor, I'm frightened!

Women's Voices

Oh, oh, what's that monster?

GLASHA

I'm surprised at you, Prokhor, what a time to play the fool!

Voices

Just like Domna: she used to live here once upon a time, so the old men say. Domna the Murderess, with a face like a catfish. It's Prokhor wearing her cloak.

SIDOR

What's got into you, Prokhor? That's not like you! This is no time to play tricks!
    Meanwhile KOSTYGA *stops clowning, picks up the second pistol, hides behind the table and, as from behind a parapet, takes aim at the* COUNT. *A pistol shot. The candle goes out.*

MAX

Oh, help, help! Hold me up. I'm falling . . . I'm dying . . .
    Falls into the arms of the servants who have run up to him.

A Voice

Who did it?

MAX

It's Platon, the murderer. It was his turn to shoot, he said he'd do it. No, don't touch me, I'm dying. . . .

Another Voice

It couldn't have been Platon, your lordship. Platon has flown. He's gone for good.

First Voice

No one has seen Platon. He must have fired from the garden through the open window.

Third Voice

Nonsense, it was that clown in the fancy dress who fired. I saw him do it.

Second Voice

Then it must have been Prokhor. They say he was wearing that fancy dress a while back.

First Voice

It's not like Prokhor. It couldn't have been him. But why not light a candle, get hold of the clown and find out who he is!

Third Voice

You'd have to catch up with him first. Go and catch up with the wind in the fields.

First Voice

But it was not Prokhor. Look at all these people milling round. It might have been any one of them.

Voices in the distance

Lyoshka Leshakov! Lyoshka Leshakov!
A dog barks off stage. Also off stage, someone, carrying a candle, walks past the door but does not come in.

MAX

I'm very poorly my friends. The pain makes my head go round and round. My left shoulder must be broken.

SIDOR

Could it have been Prokhor? I can't believe it! Wait a minute, my lord. The four of us will carry you to her ladyship's bedroom. I know she'll be grateful to us. Then we'll send to town for a doctor. No, it couldn't have been Prokhor.

Second Voice

If the key is in the door, we must lock up. Once we've carried his lordship out, the study will be empty. Everybody's gone, there's not a soul left.

Third Voice

It's not our business. Somebody's sure to come and lock up.

GLASHA

Lusha and I are here. I'll take her to her mother. Come along, poor darling.

LUSHA

What's to become of me, Glasha dear?
Exeunt. The COUNT *is carried out of the room. A little later,* FROL *and* PAKHOM *enter;* PAKHOM *is carrying a lighted candle in a candle-stick.*

PAKHOM

Never seen anything like it! What a crazy business.

FROL

You hold on to that candle. Be careful you don't drop it and set fire to the house. That would be the last straw.

PAKHOM

Let's see if Lyoshka and Kostyga have taken the lot or if there's
something left on the table.

FROL

Mind that candle, I tell you. Hold it properly. Why is your
hand shaking like that, are you drunk or something?

PAKHOM

Not like Khort, you mean? There he stands in the doorway
and doesn't bat an eyelid. Look at him staring at us like an
idol. If a dumb animal could speak, goodness knows what
tales he'd tell. To think of it makes your blood run cold.

FROL

Don't you worry about Khort. He'll be no trouble. Just mind
you don't start telling tales yourself. Or I'll show you, you cur.
Your own mother won't know you! So just watch out!

PAKHOM

I saw you making signs to Kostyga.

FROL

Signs? I'll give you signs! I'll crush you like a gnat. I'll beat the
life out of you. You'll remember it to the end of your days,
damn you. Don't you dare breathe a word.

PAKHOM

Where's the casket?

FROL

All right, I'll tell you, your excellency. It's in the same place
where I'm sending you tomorrow to help push the daisies up.

PAKHOM

Is that the way to talk to your friend.

FROL

My friend, are you? Tell that to the birds in the trees!

PAKHOM

So you really mean to go to Straton, to call the soldiers?

FROL

Yes, I do – I'm going straight away, you nitwit. And I'll bring back witnesses and magistrates and soldiers. There'll be such a to-do here tomorrow, you won't believe it. You'll be staggered at the turn I'm going to give this thing. As for you and me, we'll let bygones be bygones. Stick by me and you won't be sorry. I'll be such a good friend to you that you'll need the rest of your life to pray for me.

PAKHOM

All right. I've got other things to think about. I'm heartbroken for Lusha.

SCENE TWO

*

Fifteen years later. A bench outside a forester's hut. Summer. Woods all around.

PAKHOM

Good day to you. We were told to expect you. Her ladyship has promised to be here soon. If you would wait here for her. Do you understand our language at all?

LIEUTENANT RIMMARS

A little.

PAKHOM

Good. Then we're sure to manage. Here comes her ladyship. Walking straight through the woods.
    Enter Elena.
My humble greetings, my lady. Here's an officer from foreign parts waiting for you.

ELENA

Thank you, Pakhom. Leave us now. Wait somewhere not too near.

PAKHOM

Yes, my lady. And in case anything should happen, I'll whistle. You don't want to land in a mess.

ELENA

All right, Pakhom.

Exit PAKHOM. ELENA *and the* LIEUTENANT *embrace and cling to each other for a long time. They are so moved that for some minutes they can't even speak.*

ELENA

How many years since we last met?

RIMMARS

It was twelve years ago!

ELENA

I make it fourteen.

RIMMARS

Yes, it's true. Indeed it's fifteen. I was wrong.

ELENA

They wrote to me that you are an officer now and that you've changed your name.

RIMMARS

Yes, I'm a lieutenant in the Engineers. They call me Rimmars: it means fugitive or stranger.

ELENA

And you have learnt their language so well and in so short a time?

RIMMARS

Let's sit on the bench.

ELENA

How do you say that in Swedish?

RIMMARS

Var so god och sit.

ELENA

Goodness, what a long sentence! It's longer than the bench. *(Laughs.)*

RIMMARS

Our King was one of Napoleon's generals, but in 1812 he sided with Russia. The population is fairly small and they welcome foreigners. It's an honour to be a soldier, and I greatly enjoy it.

ELENA

What's the Swedish for forest?

RIMMARS

Skog.

ELENA

And forester?

RIMMARS

Skogwachtor – you'd say, Skogwachtor Pakhom Surepyev.

ELENA

So you recognised him?

RIMMARS

Of course I did.

ELENA

And did he know you?

RIMMARS

Yes, certainly. But he thinks he's not supposed to, so he's willing to pretend he doesn't.

ELENA

Does it surprise you that I ask you such silly questions? Oh, if only we could spend our whole lives like this, sitting side by side on this bench and talking nonsense. What a forest is in Swedish and things like that. And saying yes and no. What bliss to have such simple needs: like sitting in the sun and enjoying the scent of the new grass.

RIMMARS

I hear you are married to the young Count. And that you have children – two girls and a boy.

ELENA

Yes. Let me tell you everything from the beginning. You'll want to hear about poor Max. He didn't die of his bullet wound that night. He recovered and lived for two more years.

RIMMARS

What did he die of?

ELENA

A bad chill. He soon forgave me and dissuaded me from going into a convent. Things began to get better on the estate even during his lifetime. He seemed to become wiser, more sensible. But the real change came when his heir, Iriney Norovtsev, inherited the property.

RIMMARS

I remember Iriney as a child. It seems he has lived up to the hopes they had of him. Everyone used to praise him for his kindness.

ELENA

He manages the estate wonderfully. Lots of new farm buildings have gone up. And new houses in the villages. We help the peasants.

RIMMARS

You have built a theatre, too, they say.

ELENA

Yes, it holds three hundred people. It's famous all over Russia.

RIMMARS

I'd even heard about it abroad.

ELENA

There's a special reason why the theatre means a lot to me. I'll tell you why later.

RIMMARS

And I heard that most of the peasants pay rent instead of working for the master.

ELENA

Iriney is sure that it won't be long before all the serfs in Russia will be freed by Imperial decree. They say there's already a committee working on it in secret.

RIMMARS

I heard rumours of it abroad.

ELENA

Well, now, you wanted to know about my marriage. Iriney
kept asking for my hand for a long time. At first I refused, then
I ended by accepting. He is a good man, he loves me. We have
children.

RIMMARS

And what about our son?

ELENA

He is growing up as Lusha Agafonov's child. I couldn't do
anything else.

RIMMARS

I know.

ELENA

Max was still alive, of course. He knew that he couldn't have
children. And that wild night still hadn't been forgotten. He
hadn't yet forgiven me. I was living on my own in our god-
forsaken little town, so I took Lusha to live with me. She was
given her freedom just after she had lost her sight. If you
remember, she was already with child. A month later, so was I.
There was only about a couple of months' between us. Well,
one day Lusha, because of her blindness, tripped up on the
steps and had a miscarriage. When I had my child, Lusha
agreed to take it and pretend it was hers – we all but suckled
him together. So you can imagine what a fine child he grew to
be. We lived quietly, on our own. We got away with it. No
one suspects anything. Not even Lusha s husband, Trofim
Agafonov, has guessed. Anyway Lusha and he have parted,
he's a soldier and he doesn t live with her when he comes on
leave.

RIMMARS

And how is Lusha herself?

ELENA

She's been with me ever since then. She is dearer to me than a sister.

RIMMARS

But what about her eyes? Can she see at all?

ELENA

Only a sort of faint blur. There was one doctor who gave us some hope. He said he could cure her and was ready to start.

RIMMARS

Well then, why the delay?

ELENA

She wouldn't go to him. She's afraid he'll make her worse. But sooner or later we'll try, of course.

RIMMARS

And the boy?

ELENA

Our son?

RIMMARS

How is he growing up? What is he like?

ELENA

Exactly as I said he would be. I suppose you've forgotten.

That night when I told you there was no sin between us
yet – that there could only be sin when I bore you a child,
a little madcap for all the world to wonder at – and then I
corrected myself and said that even then there would be no
sin.

RIMMARS

Let me see him just once, give me that joy.

ELENA

You can see him before I do, if you like. He's studying in
Paris together with Pakhom's grand-daughter Stepanida
Surepyev, and several other of our village boys and girls.

RIMMARS

Do you mean to say that sort of thing is still done? Is it to
make painters or actors of them?

ELENA

They are being trained as a troupe for our theatre.

RIMMARS

And they are all serfs?

ELENA

Oh, but don't you see, it's only in name. Their position is
exactly the same as though they were free.

RIMMARS

And your son is one of them?

ELENA

But everyone thinks he's Agafonov's.

RIMMARS

And you put up with this?

ELENA

He is growing up under my care. I'll never let him come to any harm. As for his being a serf, it's only a word, it doesn't mean anything.

RIMMARS

What about his self-respect? Your other children are growing up as the Count's, aren't they?

ELENA

But he doesn't know he is their brother. God forbid he should find out.

RIMMARS

Why doesn't the Count grant their freedom to all those who have been sent abroad to become actors?

ELENA

If he did that, they would all scatter. That would be the end of our theatre. It's his great passion, you see. He doesn't care what he spends on training them. They are being taught by the very best French actors – Anna Mars, Bresson, Dupont. And our boy is the most outstanding of them all! Such brains, fire, courage, talent! He was christened Dimitri, but his companions have nicknamed him Fortune, and the name has stuck.

RIMMARS

And Prokhor? Is he alive?

F

ELENA

Ah, that's still an open wound.

RIMMARS

What happened? He didn't die, did he? I heard he's his own
master now, doing very well for himself.

ELENA

That's true, but at what a price! He bought his freedom at the
cost of terrible beatings, his skin was hanging in shreds.

RIMMARS

I knew he'd suffered, and done forced labour.

ELENA

They put all the blame on him. They said it was he who had
fired at the Count and stolen the jewels. That fancy dress
played a fateful part in all this affair. It was just his luck that he
had tried it on earlier. When they saw the other man clowning
around in it later, they all shouted it was Prokhor.

RIMMARS

He was innocent and he alone was blamed?

ELENA

That's what gives me no peace. I knew he couldn't have had
anything to do with it, but I could not stand up for him. I
allowed him to be tortured, I kept silent, I let it happen. That
will never be forgiven me in the next world.

RIMMARS

He was sentenced to a terrible number of strokes?

ELENA

Two thousand. That was in place of the death sentence he had received at first.

RIMMARS

It's astonishing that he survived, that they didn't beat him to death.

ELENA

The two thousand strokes were to be administered in four goes but each time he collapsed before he had received five hundred lashes; so they took him to hospital to recover and then gave him the next lot. Then, after this torture, he was sentenced to penal servitude for life and sent to Siberia. But after Max s death, when Iriney came into the estate, we at once started proceedings to prove his innocence.

RIMMARS

His case was reviewed?

ELENA

Yes, but what difficulties we had! And what a long time it took!

RIMMARS

The usual official delays?

ELENA

Yes, just try and fight our Government clerks. And that wasn't the only thing. You remember Straton, who was District Inspector when you were here?

RIMMARS

How could I forget his worship. A bloated nonentity with a
pig's snout and slits for eyes.

ELENA

Well, he's our Chief of Police now, and I wouldn't be surprised
if he soon becomes Governor. He started as a batman, an
uncouth illiterate lout, but living amongst lick-spittles he
began to see himself as a brilliant wit and lady-killer. Ignorant
fool that he is, he naturally took a dislike to the whole Norovtsev
family, simply because of their breeding – for what he called
their fancy ways. He can't leave women alone and, naturally,
they don't refuse him. Unfortunately, he tried it with me and
was staggered when I turned him down. But all this is nothing.
What matters now is that the emancipation of the serfs is really
in the air at last. Iriney is one of the moving spirits behind it, he
has made a serious study of the problem, he is always writing
about it to pass on what he knows. Straton, who is of peasant
origin himself but now an upstart landowner, is all for serfdom
and against emancipation. Because he hated us so much, he put
obstacles in our way when we were trying to get Prokhor's
sentence revised. But ten years ago the bandit Kostyga was
caught and the evidence he gave before he died definitely
cleared Prokhor. His innocence was established and he was
released. Iriney gave him his freedom, and money to set
himself up. Prokhor got a Government licence to sell spirits.
You ought to go and see him unless you're afraid to let it be
known that you are back. It's quite near here. He keeps an
inn and a posting station on the highway. He is thrifty and
businesslike. I'd say, his position in the district is second only to
the Count's. We treat him almost as an equal. Straton, for all
his swagger and his top boots, has nothing like his power and
influence.

The sound of a whistle off stage.

RIMMARS

That's Pakhom's signal.

ELENA

Yes, you must go. Hurry.

RIMMARS

I'll be around here for another week. I'll drop in on Prokhor. It would be nice if we could meet again before I leave for good.

ELENA

We must. I'll let you know. I'll find a way.
Another whistle, nearer and louder.
Go quickly. Don't let's say goodbye! Run!
RIMMARS *hurries away.* ELENA *follows him with her eyes as she talks to herself.*
Goodbye, a happy journey to you, my bright falcon. I haven't told you how much I miss you. You will never hear me say that. Why should I torment you to no purpose? But how splendid you are, my love. It's my longing for you that has raised you above all others. It's my thoughts and prayers for you that have lifted you to such a height, my treasure, my pride. And yet I can look my husband honestly in the eyes – I am not deceiving him, I can see all that is good and noble in him, I am not betraying his name. You will ask me why things have turned out so wrong? Find me a life that's gone right. No wonder people say: 'Don't live as you wish, but as God ordains'. And I thank you, Lord, my great shield and protector, for ordaining that I should live to such inscrutable ends, a life so full of difficulties and confusion; for ordaining that my

heart should bleed so sweetly. It's only the Stratons with their eyes buried in fat who imagine that life was given us for pleasure, and who strut about in their creaking jackboots, and lay down the law and preach and impose order on others. But life is a dagger-thin pain that illuminates the spirit, a quiet gift of bright yet silent power, a long-lasting power, such as they have never dreamed of.

Enter PAKHOM.

PAKHOM

You'd better hide in the forest too, your ladyship. You don't want to get into more trouble, God forbid.

ELENA

What happened? Why did you whistle?

PAKHOM

It's His Excellency, Straton – crashing like a wild boar straight through the forest.

ELENA

It's time for me to go home anyway. Only don't imagine I'm going because of him. I'm not afraid of that scarecrow.

PAKHOM

Who would ever think such a thing, my lady? You've simply been for a walk and you're going home. You do as you please, my lady. (*Exit* ELENA, *soon after enters* STRATON.)

STRATON

Who was that making off downhill through the hazelwood? I called out, but the swine took no notice, just made off into the gulley. Am I expected to run after him or what?

PAKHOM

That certainly wouldn't do. You'd only get out of breath.
That was Platon Shcheglov, who used to be a serf in Pyatibratskoye, till he got away. He's turned up in these parts again,
come to visit the neighbourhood.

STRATON

Then why didn't you catch him and tie him up, you oaf...

PAKHOM

And how could I lay hands on him, your excellency, when he is
now an officer from a foreign country?

STRATON

Yes, that would make it difficult. I suppose he was making
love to your mistress?

PAKHOM

Good Lord no, excellency! How could they undress in the
open? They just talked in a friendly way. All very decent and
proper.

STRATON

Good, good. I'll keep that in mind.

ACT ONE

The Middle Part of the Play

*

SCENE ONE

The year 1860. Interior of a peasant hut, neglected, dark, untidy. End of a winter night. Raging snowstorm outside.

PAKHOM

(lying on the stove, sighing, groaning and calling out): What is all this, God forgive me. Can this be the end? Can it be time for me to die! I'm dying. I'm dying.

MARFA

(lying on a bench below and waking up with a start): Oh Lord, it's the end. As God is my witness, it's the end!

PAKHOM

What d'you mean, the end? The end of what? What are you so pleased about, you old fool?

MARFA

I was saying the night is nearly ended. It's nearly dawn.

PAKHOM

Dawn, you silly fool! It's me that's finished, your Pakhom, I'm dying. Dawn indeed! It's my hour that's come, mother, it's my death that's on the doorstep. What we need is a priest.

MARFA

What are you talking about, father? What do you mean, your hour? God bless you, you're half asleep, you're dreaming. Just listen to what goes on outside. The blizzard is as bad as ever.

PAKHOM

We ought to send for the priest, I tell you, for Father Onufriy. I want to confess. Don't stand there, staring and gaping. D'you think I'm joking? With a fool of a woman like you, a man could land in the next world without the last sacraments.

MARFA

Don't talk like that. It's just something that's come over you, a fancy you've got into your head. Nobody dies like that, all of a sudden, without warning. Last night, there you were, mending the harness and lifting sacks that weigh forty pounds, and now suddenly you talk about having the last sacraments and dying.

PAKHOM

I've been bad before but I always got over it. This time it's different, I can feel it, it's the end. It's as though there were a leaden weight crushing me.

MARFA *leaves* PAKHOM'S *side, busies herself at the back of the hut, splits twigs for kindling, gets the fire going in the stove and comes back.*

MARFA

Be sensible, Pakhom. There's such a snowstorm that nobody could get through by sledge or on foot. We're beside the lake, the bank slopes sheer down below the window. At this season, in mid-winter, it should be frozen over, but just look at what's going on. The ice is breaking up as though it were St. George's day, and floating away from the shore. You tell me to go and fetch the priest – am I to swim across the lake like a grey duck? And if I walk round it, I wouldn't get there till tomorrow night. And another thing you have to get into your head – it's snowing so hard that we've hardly seen God's daylight for three days past. Father Onufriy will never come out in weather like this.

She moves away again, fusses about at the back of the house and comes back.

I'll tell you what, Pakhom dear. You should get up, you might feel better. Once you are on your feet you will get over it. Heave yourself up, lean on me, I'll help you. Why don't you answer me, Pakhom? Say something, dear, you're frightening me. Oh Lord, Oh what a fool I am! I thought he'd been lying on his back too long. I thought I'd rub it, so he'd feel better, but now he's lying there lifeless. Can he really have gone, my Pakhom? Oh Lord, what a misfortune! It's true, he's gone to his Maker.

She starts wailing, as over the dead.

Why have you left me, who'll look after me, now you're gone, my mainstay, my protector. You're leaving me in torment, you've gone from me, my shield, my fortress. What have I done wrong? How have I lost your love? I've not looked after you, I've let you go, I couldn't keep you.

PAKHOM

(*comes to*): I thought I was going. I moved my arm, and the pain took my breath away. It hurts so much, I can't bear it. Thank goodness I've come to, or I'd have died without telling you. Stop wailing now. You'll have time to weep afterwards. Don't torment me, listen to me. Down in the foundations of the barn, there's a brick I've marked, it's the fifth from the corner. You must find it and take it out, and dig about a bit – take out all the other bricks around it. Do it at night so that no one sees you, and put them all back in the morning. When you find the hollow, you'll see for yourself. I was putting the stuff aside to buy us our freedom. But now you'll get your freedom for nothing. They'll give you a plot of land. Buy a little more besides, and buy another horse. Oh, it's come again, I can't bear it any more. I can't breathe. I can't feel my arms and legs.

He loses consciousness once more and MARFA *again bursts into sobs.*

MARFA

Take me too, dear God! Take your servant, now my strength and my hope is gone.

PAKHOM

(*coming to again*): We must say goodbye, Marfa dear. It's time. If we don't, it will be too late. Forgive me, for the love of Christ, forgive me all the grumbling, the blows, forget your tears and my hard words.

MARFA

Don't, don't my dear. I'm no saint that you should ask my forgiveness. You've never sinned against me, and I don't bear you any grudge.

PAKHOM

Thank you, for forgetting all the thrashings, all the swearing. It takes some of the weight off my soul. As for my other lies and sins, the thieving, the dishonesty, those only God can forgive. That's what I wanted the priest for. I'd have told him all my crimes, I'd have confessed. I can't bring myself to tell you. It was through Frol Dryagin that I brought damnation on my soul. It was Frol, the devil, that bound me hand and foot with his terrible secret.

MARFA

That's enough, father. The world is full of evil. We're all born in wickedness. God alone is without sin.

PAKHOM

It's my fault that Lusha had such a cross to bear, that she's lived in darkness and in suffering.

MARFA

What are you saying, Pakhom? What are you thinking of? Who are we to judge if God's punishment is just?

PAKHOM

What was the name of that dog the master had? I'm beginning to lose my memory.

MARFA

Which dog, bless you? Or can it really be that your mind is wandering?

PAKHOM

Lyoshka Leshakov was done away with by his own men – he knew too much. Kostyga, they say, died in prison. Yet what were those two as compared to Frol? Nothing but children.

MARFA

You must be feeling a bit better, Pakhom dear, you seem livelier now you've got talking.

PAKHOM

It was one thing after another. First the conscripts going off. Then their running away from the recruiting office and deserting. Then the attack on our master, God rest him, and the robbery, and the wandering about from place to place. It was Frol, that wicked devil, who made me hold my tongue when the police started their inquiry at Sumtsovo. There was weeping and wailing and gnashing of teeth. Soldiers took over the estate, people were beaten with sticks and rifle butts. And through our fault, because we did not speak, an innocent man was nearly beaten to death.

MARFA

You're still thinking of Prokhor? He had a lot to bear, I don't say he didn't – tortured and dragged in chains to Siberia. But think of all the luck he had afterwards! All the happiness his suffering brought him! Free as a Cossack, and with his own inn. Some of those horses of his would be the envy of the Tsar's posting stations, and his power in the district is second only to the Count's.

PAKHOM

Khort, he was called, that dog. Now I remember. Frightening he was, as black as a devil. When he stood up on his hind legs and put his front paws on your chest, you daren't breathe or there'd be trouble. That happened one day to Gideon, the mechanic, the father of the tutor at the big house. He lost his head and ran. Khort went after him and savaged him to death. I do seem to be feeling a little better, you're right. I'm going to try to lift myself up on my elbow and turn over.

He makes an awkward movement, cries out, falls back and faints. Outside, someone goes by with a lantern which swings up and down, lighting up the snowdrifts along the road. Re-peated knocking on the door.

MARFA

Can the Lord have heard Pakhom's prayer and sent us Father Onufiy? Who could it be at such an hour?
The knocking grows louder, then the door is pulled violently and flung open. Enter FROL, *the village elder, and the policeman* SHOKHIN.

FROL

Locking yourselves up like newly-weds! We knocked and knocked. Here's Shokhin, our new constable. He knows no-body yet, so I'm taking him from house to house, showing him round. These are the Surepyevs. You can put out the lantern, they've got a rush-light. Anyway, it's nearly morning. Put two crosses in the register, to show that the two Surepyevs are present and correct. Come on, you two, put your sheepskins on, get your spades and come and shovel the snow off the road like everybody else. Road duty. Let's go on, Shokhin. What are you howling for, Marfa?
MARFA *sobs and can't get out a word.*
Stop it. Quiet! Aren't you ashamed of yourself, crying over such a trifling thing? If I started letting people off, how would we ever get the road cleared? I'm not asking you to cart water. Just to shovel snow off the road – that's not asking much, is it?
MARFA *mumbles unintelligibly through her sobs.*
Stop crying. They say you'll soon be free now. Can't you do just that much for your master, one last time? You've got to understand – it's carnival week. After that, all through Lent there won't be any theatricals at the Count's. These are the last until after Easter. What you've got to get into your head is that a lot of guests have been invited. At the posting station at

Lesnoye, they say there's a string of sleighs and carriages a mile long – all held up. It doesn't bear thinking about. Horses sinking into the snow. There are even some guests who've come from abroad. But I forgot who I was talking to. You should know: isn't the leading lady, Stepanida, a grand-daughter of yours? Oh well! All right! I'll let you off. You can stay at home and God bless you. Only stop crying, will you. Cross her off the list. Pakhom can go by himself. Where's he hiding? I don't seem to see him.

MARFA

(*sobbing*): He's dying, poor lamb, he's dying.

FROL

I've heard that one before. You're all ill or dying on a week-day, but you come out of your coffins on Sundays.

MARFA

How you can scoff at us in that ungodly way. As if all we had to think about was shamming illness to get out of working for the master. No wonder my poor Pakhom warned me against you, no wonder he told me to shun you like the plague!

FROL

Warned you against me, did he? Fancy that now. What did he say, I wonder?

MARFA

Run and call the priest, Marfa, he said – I must make my confession before I die and tell him all about that devil, Frol.

FROL

Did he now?

MARFA

It was when the police started the inquiry at Sumtsovo, he said . . .

FROL

(*interrupting her sharply*): Wait! Don't go so fast. Wait, I tell you. I've got to have a word with the constable.
To SHOKHIN.
Instead of standing about doing nothing, why don't you take the list and go on with your round? Get the whole village out. I'll just finish with her and catch up with you.

SHOKHIN

What about the man, Pakhom? Shall I cross him off too?

FROL

Might as well, I reckon.
Exit SHOKHIN.
Well, go on now, talk. And mind you don't tell me any lies. What is it he said to you about me?

MARFA

During the inquiry at Sumtsovo, he said . . .

FROL

What inquiry was that, you silly woman? You keep on about it, but there was no such thing. It's the first I've heard of it. Well, all right, that's enough of your cackle. Better tell me where he is, your poor sick lamb. Let me see him. I won't eat him up. If he's really at death's door, I must ask his forgiveness, take leave of him and kiss him for the last time. And if it isn't true, so much the better. Perhaps I can help him, get

him on his feet. You'll never know how to thank me enough
then.

PAKHOM

(*recovering consciousness*): I must have fainted again. How long
have I been like this? Who's that talking to you, Marfa? It's not
the priest by any chance, turned up by good luck?

MARFA

It's Frol, talk of the devil.

FROL

It's me, Pakhom. It's Frol, your old and faithful friend.

PAKHOM

Get out of here! Out of my sight, you spawn of Satan. Don't
touch me. Let me die in peace.

FROL

You're rambling, Pakhom. Don't you see who I am? Better
let me come up there, I'll ease you up very gently and help
you to your feet.
   *Climbs on to a bench so that his shoulders are level with the top
   of the stove, does something there.*

PAKHOM

Let me alone! What are you doing, you brute? You're hurting
me!

FROL

(*from above*): Well, it seems you were right, I can't get him up
after all. He's too weak. He's got a rattle in his throat. He keeps
falling back like a sack.

G

Coming down, after a moment.
He's gone to his Maker. May he rest in peace.
Crosses himself.

MARFA

(*sobbing loudly again, speaks through her tears*): And did you help him on his way, you killer, you fiend?

ACT ONE

*

SCENE TWO

Morning. Posting station of Lesnoye, the day after PAKHOM'S *death. Waiting room for travellers. It stretches from up-stage left diagonally to the back and is divided by an archway supported by two columns. At the back of the waiting room, beyond the archway, is the entrance lobby and three windows facing the street. Up-stage left, sitting at a table and writing in his notebook, is* ALEXANDRE DUMAS (PÈRE), *the French writer who is travelling through Russia.* SASHA VET-KHOPESHCHERNIKOV *enters from the back, looks round in search of* DUMAS *and goes up to him.*

SASHA

Monsieur Dumas, if I'm not mistaken?

DUMAS

Yes, that is my name. May I ask you in my turn with whom I have the honour of speaking?

SASHA

I am tutor to the children of the Norovtsev family.

DUMAS

I am all the more delighted to make your acquaintance. Do sit down. I can guess what you have come to tell me: that the festivities have been put off?

SASHA

Not a bit of it. The Count has asked me to set your mind completely at rest. You are eagerly awaited. The performances will take place as soon as communications have been restored.

DUMAS

There was a rumour that we might be able to move on today.

SASHA

I am not quite so hopeful as that. The roads are in a very bad state.

DUMAS

That's what the station master told me. By the way, I have the impression that I've seen him before, yet this is the first time I've ever been to Russia, apart from a brief visit to the French front during the Crimean campaign. At that time I was a correspondent for several Paris newspapers to which I sent dispatches from the theatre of war. Well, as I was saying, this station master, who so much reminds me of someone – we offered to pay him double if he would take us quickly on our way. But he refused point blank. I'm a government official, he said, I have no right to risk damaging the sleighs and horses belonging to the state. It appears, however, that there is someone near here, a private citizen, the landlord of an inn on the highway, who has offered to help us in our predicament.

SASHA

In that case you are very lucky. This must be Prokhor Medvedev – he is a man of his word.

DUMAS

He suggested that we should move to his inn, and he promised to get us to our destination with all possible comfort and speed.

SASHA

If he has promised, he'll do it. His coachmen drive at breakneck speed, and he has fiery horses, that go like the wind. Apart from that, when it gets about that Medvedev has offered you his services, the road will be cleared much faster.

DUMAS

Do the local peasants think so highly of him?

SASHA

This man was tortured, flogged to within an inch of his life, sent to Siberia in chains and came back ten years later when it was found that there had been a miscarriage of justice. He has bought the independence he enjoys, his prestige and his practical experience at the price of inhuman suffering.

DUMAS

I can guess who he is. Many people, both in Moscow and Petersburg, have told me about Pyatibratskoye and the so-called Sumtsovo affair which was once the talk of the country. This man must surely be that famous servant of the Count, and the Countess's lover, who shot and wounded her husband.

SASHA

No, that's not the one. The man of whom you speak fled abroad and, from what we have heard, took service in Sweden. The one who was blamed for all the crimes committed that night was Prokhor, though he was the only one who had tried to prevent them.

DUMAS

Shall I find Countess Norovtsev on her estate? Or is she away? I am eager to make her acquaintance. By all accounts she must be about fifty, but they say she looks much younger.

SASHA

The Countess died last year.

DUMAS

I had no idea. What caused her to die before her time? Was she happy with her second husband?

SASHA

Immensely. Almost too happy. I think that what brought her to an early grave was her excessive concern for the needs and interests of Pyatibratskoye – she had been quite indifferent to them during her first marriage, but in recent years she took them too much to heart. She could not resign herself to the envy and hostility of various upstarts and of some neighbours which, almost by tradition, surround the Norovtsev family.

DUMAS

How strange. I would never have thought it. So far as I could judge, both the simple people here at the posting station, and the nobility in Moscow and Petersburg feel the greatest possible sympathy and respect for the Norovtsevs and their way of running their estate. His Majesty's Aide-de-Camp, General Oblepikhin, as well as the chief patron of your free-thinkers and lovers of liberty, Grand Duke Oleg Alexandrovich – both of them friends of the Count from his days at the Cadet Corps – are expected to pass through here on their way to attend the performances at Pyatibratskoye. In what circles or among what classes do you find those people who are hostile to the Norovt-sevs?

SASHA

Russia is not ruled by Tsars but by kennel keepers, village policemen, sergeants who have risen to be chiefs of police, tenth grade government officials. It's the ignorant provincial satraps who dislike the Norovtsev family. That martinet, Straton Nalyotov, used to pester Countess Elena with his attentions. His vanity was wounded by the contempt with which she turned him down, and he took his revenge by persecuting whole communities in the neighbourhood. This too must have contributed to the shortening of her life. Other people who dislike the Norovtsevs are certain idlers and gossips, who were once adored by their female cousins and aunts on the neighbouring estates and who go on scrounging on them for the rest of their lives. Some of these failed geniuses still manage to throw dust into people's eyes and they hate the Norovtsevs who see through them and are not so easily impressed.

DUMAS

Can you tell me more about the Sumtsovo affair?

SASHA

I was expecting you to ask that.

DUMAS

It's only natural. There was so much talk about it at the time.

SASHA

If you are a connoisseur of horrors, mysteries and inexplicable events, you will find crimes in the past history of Pyatibratsoyek which far outshine those at Sumtsovo. What took place that night – the events later known as the Sumtsovo affair – marks the borderline between the old legends and the new state of affairs. It was that night that the new foundations were laid. The change for the better is being brought about by the more prominent inhabitants of Pyatibratskoye. The whole of the Count's family is among them, but there are three other notable figures. One of them we have already mentioned – he is the innkeeper, Prokhor.

> *To the head of the posting station,* SELIVERST KUBYNKO, *who comes up to him, limping on his wooden leg.*

What is it, Captain?

KUBYNKO

I'm in a dither, Sasha. A messenger has just arrived from the next posting station. He says His Highness the Grand Duke is already on his way. He'll be here any moment. I remember him from Sebastopol.

DUMAS

Did this man mention Sebastopol just now – or am I mistaken?

SASHA

You are right. He did.

KUBYNKO

Where can I have seen this traveller before? I suppose it's not the first time he's been through here . . . You can't remember all the faces, there are so many. Well, I must go. I mustn't waste time. What with His Highness the Grand Duke coming . . .

> *Exit.*

SASHA

We were talking of the people who are making Pyatibratskoye what it is today. There's the one I've already mentioned, the innkeeper Prokhor. Another is a member of the Count's private theatre troup – Agafonov, a remarkably gifted actor. His companions have nicknamed him Fortune. You will see him on the stage here.

DUMAS

I greatly look forward to it, and not only because I have heard a lot about him – I met him in Paris through a friend of mine, the actor Bresson. Agafonov was his favourite pupil.

SASHA

The third person, although now absent and out of reach, is very closely linked with the history of the estate. He was once a serf of the Norovtsevs and – according to some people, though others deny it – had a love affair with the Countess; he ran away and took service in Sweden under the assumed name of Everst Rimmars.

DUMAS

Everst Rimmars! How extraordinary! I met him in the Crimea. He was one of the liaison officers who represented Sweden, as a neutral country, at the French Headquarters. I met him often and got to know him well. I realised he was Russian, but I had no idea that he had such a fascinating and unusual background. He obtained the release of many Russian prisoners of war, got wounded Russians admitted into our hospitals, and saved many lives in various other ways.

SASHA

Yes, we heard about that. The station master here, Kubynko,

a retired staff captain, is one of those whom Rimmars saved.

DUMAS

Now I understand! That's why his face struck me as so familiar. Of course. I've seen him before! I used to visit our field hospitals with Rimmars and I saw this wounded Russian officer lying in one of them, after his leg had been amputated. I remember that he and Everst had a long talk and were delighted to find that they both came from the same part of the country. . . . But to change the subject – I'm amazed at how well you speak French.

SASHA

That's not unusual here, among educated people or those who have grown up on the estates of rich landowners, among the children of the gentry.
   From the back of the waiting-room a distant relation of Count Norovtsev, young KSENOFONT NOROVTSEV, *comes forward in conversation with a chance stage-coach companion, Ensign* KOLYA CHERNOUSOV.

SASHA

There's that endless talker, that trumpet of Jericho, a relation of the Count's – he's sure to come up to us and interrupt our conversation. Couldn't you look as if you were very busy taking notes, and I'll bury myself in a book – I see you have several interesting new ones there on the table.

CHERNOUSOV

Thank you, Count. But what have I done to deserve your confidence? You really shouldn't trust the first person you meet, you know.

KSENOFONT

I liked you from the moment I set eyes on you, Ensign.

CHERNOUSOV

I beg you not to call me Ensign, you touch on a raw spot.

KSENOFONT

I took an instant liking to you, Ensign. Let's exchange baptismal crosses. I know you said you had been posted somewhere, but I'm sorry, I can't remember the name of your regiment.

CHERNOUSOV

The Guards, the Grodno Hussars. But I beg you again – couldn't we avoid this subject? It brings circumstances to my mind which I would sooner forget.

KSENOFONT

I'll be like a brother to you. I'll look after your future, I'll see to everything. It's only right that brothers should devote themselves to the same cause. A distant relation, a sort of uncle of mine, Count Iriney Norovtsev is well known as the Chairman of that committee – you know the one – the Provincial committee for what's its name . . . oh, hang it . . . for peasant affairs.

CHERNOUSOV

The Committee for the Improvement of the Conditions of Agricultural Workers.

KSENOFONT

The Improvement of the Conditions of Agricultural Workers, that's right. Not that the actual name of the committee matters. The point is that it is working for the emancipation of the peasants from serfdom.

CHERNOUSOV

Exactly.

KSENOFONT

Are you familiar with the work of Monsieur Fourier, Ensign?

CHERNOUSOV

My name is Kolya, do call me that, Count.

KSENOFONT

Take for instance *The Organisation of Labour and its Remuneration*, that's the title of one of his books. In future there won't be any more exhausting or degrading work. Every human activity will be pleasurable.

CHERNOUSOV

What a delightful prospect! But are we really to believe in it?

KSENOFONT

It has been proved possible. You should keep abreast of scientific developments, you should read more, Ensign.

CHERNOUSOV

When I spoke of a delightful prospect, I was thinking of those future pleasurable activities, but not of the sad case of my military rank, of which you continue so pitilessly to remind me.

KSENOFONT

I want you to dedicate yourself fully to my ideal. That the serfs will be emancipated is certain, the decision has already been taken. The only question is when the Imperial decree will be proclaimed. But all these committees, like the one of which my uncle is chairman, for instance, are completely on the wrong track. Their proposals are based on the idea that the individual peasant will buy his right to freedom of movement and be assigned a plot of land. In other words, on the idea that a new type of peasant landowner will emerge – people who in future will turn into greedy speculators. But you don't seem to be listening.

CHERNOUSOV

On the contrary, I am hanging on your every word.

KSENOFONT

The point is, why should Russia follow a course which has already brought Western civilisation to a dead end? Why should we fall into the same mistakes as other countries? The communal forms of landholding which survive among our peasants suggest a better solution. The structure of the emancipated village should be based on the traditional village commune, the 'Mir'. That tradition should be treasured and maintained. But I can see you are trying to tell me something.

CHERNOUSOV

I am unfamiliar with the finer points of agrarian economy. I have my own troubles, Count: I told you about them, but you seem to have forgotten. When I left the Cadet Corps as an Ensign, I was given five hundred roubles of government money for my equipment. I even hoped to save a hundred of it for my mother – I'm on my way to her now.

KSENOFONT

And you've spent the lot?

CHERNOUSOV

Please, just a moment, one thing at a time.

KSENOFONT

Down to the last penny?

CHERNOUSOV

It never occurred to me to keep the five hundred separate from my own money and it got all mixed up. I'm not an accountant, after all! It's true that I've got somebody in the district who may possibly help me – a distant connection. I think he was my mother's guardian or something. He's a very influential person, but a fearful martinet, a real terror. He's the head of the local police, Straton Nalyotov.

KSENOFONT

You mean to say that drunken lout is a relation of yours?

CHERNOUSOV

Well, I wouldn't speak of him in quite those terms.

KSENOFONT

Don't talk to me about that blood-sucker, and don't go near him. All this business – your embezzlement, your career, and so on and so forth – we'll fix it all up quite differently. You'll come with me to Pyatibratskoye, I'll introduce you to my uncle. He is kindness itself. Not that he hasn't got a temper. When he gets excited, he's quite capable of grabbing a large orange tree in its tub and crowning you with it, or of throwing a burning oil-lamp at you.

CHERNOUSOV

He doesn't seem to have much self-control.

Enter YEVSEY, *a young serf of* KSENOFONT'S.

KSENOFONT

What is it, Yevsey?

YEVSEY

The samovar is boiling, shall I serve tea?

KSENOFONT

Put three spoonsful into the teapot. We'll, ask everybody to tea. Get another bottle of Lord Colbert out of the hamper and un-cork it. You do like rum in your tea, don't you, my dear Kolya?

CHERNOUSOV

Certainly. That's how I always have it.

YEVSEY

Why open a new bottle? There's still an old one to finish.

KSENOFONT

(*to Yevsey*): Get the cakes, and the hors d'oeuvres, as usual. Wait a minute, where are you off to, you blockhead? Tell his Honour, the Ensign, your views on how the peasants should be given land. Ought it to be communal property or individual lots?

YEVSEY

I couldn't rightly say, your lordship. I wouldn't know.

KSENOFONT

No, don't wriggle out of it. I'm not asking you for what you're supposed to say. And you needn't pretend to be so ignorant. Tell me honestly what you think, don't be afraid. Haven't I spent hours talking to you, telling you all about it?

YEVSEY

I'm very grateful to your lordship.

KSENOFONT

There you go again!

CHERNOUSOV

Leave him alone, Count. Honestly, I'm not at all interested in
the ins and outs of agrarian reform. Rather than stuffing his
head with all that, why not let him get the tea and rum, or
the samovar might go out, or the water boil away, God
forbid.

KSENOFONT

No, why? I don't like to leave things unfinished. One should
always get to the bottom of everything. He's got to tell us
what he thinks about the coming change. Come on, Yevsey,
talk. Don't pretend to be a block of wood.

YEVSEY

If that's what you want, my lord, I'll tell you my opinion, how
can I refuse? Of course, if you look at how our fathers and
grandfathers lived, things are a lot easier and freer nowadays.
But as to letting a man leave his master and go wherever he
wants, that of course is only what the gentry talk about over
their tea and coffee, just something to please their fancy and
while away the time. Nothing of the sort will ever happen, nor
can it.

KSENOFONT

What d'you mean, it can never happen? Explain to me,
Yevsey, I don't understand.

YEVSEY

The masters will never free their serfs of their own will. It's all a mare's nest, it can't ever happen!

KSENOFONT

How can you say that when everybody's talking about it, and when I, your lawful master, tell you myself, on my honour as a Count.

YEVSEY

Well, your lordship, young gentlemen say such a lot of things, sitting in their drawing rooms. You can't believe everything. You especially, my lord, if you won't take it amiss, you're just like a little child. Somebody has only to tell you about something and there you sit with your ears flapping and take it all in and believe it, just like a simpleton, as God is my witness.

KSENOFONT

You ignorant fool, how dare you talk like that about your master!
Raises his hand to slap YEVSEY'S *face.* YEVSEY *stands at attention and makes no attempt to cover his face with his hands. People gather round, curious to see what will happen next, but* KSENOFONT *drops his arm and they wander off, disappointed. From the highway comes the sound of a coachhorn and the jingling of bells.*
Voices in the room
It's the Grand Duke!
Several people run to the windows at the back of the waiting room. KUBYNKO *crosses the room, limping on his wooden leg towards the entrance door.*

H

KSENOFONT

(*affectedly covering his face in shame*): We ought to be ashamed of ourselves! What brutes slave-owning makes of us!
Exit with CHERNOUSOV, *followed by* YEVSEY, *who goes to get the tea ready.*

DUMAS

That scene must have been very instructive. Could you please tell me what they were talking about? Who is that young man?

SASHA

I think I told you: it's Ksenofont Norovtsev, he's vaguely a nephew to the Count. He has convinced himself that he is a follower of Monsieur Fourier. That's what he was talking about. He was trying to prove that when the serfs are emancipated and are given land . . .

DUMAS

Forgive me for interrupting you. How much land?

SASHA

I don't think that's been settled yet, so I don't know exactly. It's generally assumed that it will be three to four desyatins per family.

DUMAS

That means nothing to me. How many acres is that?

SASHA

If I am not mistaken, about eight or ten. But I'm not sure.

DUMAS

That's very little. But I interrupted you. You were telling me what the young Count was saying.

SASHA

He was talking about his fear that, if the peasants are given private, independent plots of land, some of them will in time get rich and turn into greedy cannibals, vampires who will suck the blood of other peasants. He believes that the reform, if it isn't carried out properly, could undermine that sense of solidarity and collective responsibility which exists among the peasants now, living as they do in their traditional way.

DUMAS

Coming from a convinced Fourierist, such a fear is well justified. Russians seem to have a passion for social ideas. The Count raised his hand to strike his servant, but he restrained himself in time. There was something patriarchal about that scene, as though it were all in the family – though naturally, I suppose, he has freed his servant and pays him a wage.

SASHA

No, that is one of his serfs.

DUMAS

Are you telling me that a man who calls himself a disciple of Fourier is a slave-owner? What a difference between his preaching and his practice! So his convictions are not sincere?

SASHA

No, for all I know they may be perfectly genuine. But we Russians don't like wasting our time on details. Our freedom lovers are busy rescuing whole nations. They are concerned with the whole of mankind, not with individual people.

DUMAS

So their good intentions are all for show! Could anything be more revolting? I'm sorry, do forgive me. Please don't be offended.

SASHA

No, it's not hypocrisy, as you suppose. Several centuries of lack of independence, when we were dominated by the Tartars, have arrested the development of our concept of the state. Our civic sense, our feeling for normal every-day life and for personal dignity, have weakened or atrophied. On the other hand, our sense of mission and our view of the interdependence of mankind, both drawn from the Scriptures, are stronger than in any other country in the world.

DUMAS

I wonder if there is the same conflict in the mind of the Count himself? I was told that the actors and actresses who appear in his private theatre are all serfs. I find it hard to believe. How is it possible? How does it fit in with the moral standards which are ascribed to him, and with the public mission he has assumed as a champion of the liberation of the serfs? Why doesn't he free his actors – or does he, too, dislike wasting his time on trifles, and is interested only in problems on a world scale?

SASHA

You are wrong to make fun of him. The so-called corvée – the labour service owed to the landlord has long been replaced at Pyatibratskoye by an annual sum which the peasant pays for the partial right to work elsewhere and go where he likes. In other words: the peasants at Pyatibratskoye already live in the conditions which all Russian peasants will enjoy once serfdom has been abolished. As for the Count's actors, they are on an altogether special footing. He is fonder of them than of his own family. Finally, and this is the main point, as chairman of the regional committee and through his connections at court, he knows for certain that all the Russian peasants will receive their freedom in a year at most – by the Tsar's personal edict. The reason he could not introduce the reform sooner on his own estate was the opposition of his relatives, whose consent to all important measures is required by the law of entail.

From the back of the stage, in a corner hidden by the archway which perhaps conceals the refreshment bar, comes the deep, low rumble of an imperious voice; the words are indistinguishable.

DUMAS

What a pleasant intonation! That gentleman peppers his speech with French words and has a perfect Parisian accent. If that is not the Count, it must surely be some other unusual and distinguished personality.

SASHA

Nothing of the sort. That's the former landowner, Yevstigney Kortomsky, who has drunk away all he ever had. In his dubious role as connoisseur of music and the arts, he spends years on end staying with other landowners, moving from house to house. He has gambled away his land, his serfs, his house and all his goods and chattels. All he's got left are two old servants, Gury and Mavra, who've been with him ever since he was a child. They live as best they can in the ruined outhouse of an abandoned farm. They're too old to work with their hands, but they are devoted to him and have found another way of supporting him. They go out begging, supposedly without his knowledge and against his will, and thus supply him with his pocket money.

DUMAS

How is it possible? He sounds educated, a man of taste and of ideas. There's so much noise here, I can't hear him properly, but I recognised the verses he was reciting. They were part of a soliloquy from *Le Cid*. And this man takes money from beggars for his own use, quotes Corneille! It's unbelievable.

SASHA

Probably his tutor made him learn that fragment by heart when he was a child, and he still remembers it because no other bits of knowledge have come his way to dislodge that one. Perhaps he heard that you were here at the station, and recited it on purpose to impress you. But I must warn you against him, as I did against Ksenofont Norovtsev. Don't take any notice of him, pretend you don't see him, or you will have endless trouble.

GURY *and* MAVRA, *in rags and with beggars' staffs and bundles, cross the back of the stage and go up to* KORTOMSKY.

MAVRA

Thank goodness we've caught up with you in all that snow and on our tottering old legs. We were hurrying along. We saw you from far away, running up the steps to see Seliverst at the posting station. We thought we'd follow you quietly, without anybody seeing us, or they'd have been bound to stop us. Here's a muffler somebody gave us – I've brought it for you. Wrap it round your neck so you won't catch cold. You were down with the fever for a whole month at that widow's house, remember?

KORTOMSKY

(*roughly, pretending not to know them*): Where d'you think you're going? Who let you in? This place is for clean, respectable people, not for beggars covered with lice.

GURY

You don't need to drive us away, we're going, we don't want to disgrace you. Only I beg and pray you, leave that accursed drink alone, whatever it's godless name is. I can't even say it.

MAVRA

He can't say Doppel-Kümmel, he just can't.

GURY

Never mind what it's called, it's enough to give you a fit anyway. Nobody would say anything if you didn't get drunk. What does a soft-head like you know? Any lackey can drink and stay sober. But it's different with drunkards. They're as delicate as little children. They have to take care.

KORTOMSKY

(*pushing them out*): Out! Get out! You'll foul up the whole place if you get a chance. I don't know you from Adam. And I don't want to listen to your nonsense.

Unobtrusively takes a handful of coppers from them. Exeunt the beggars, MAVRA *wiping away her tears and* GURY *shaking his head.* KORTOMSKY *comes up stage and stops a few feet away from where* SASHA *and* DUMAS *are sitting in their corner. He knows that* DUMAS *is watching him. He is drunk, and clowns and shows off.*

KORTOMSKY

It's nearly Lent. A time for repentance. I'm telling you. We must pray: 'Grant us to repent, Thou who hast granted us life,' or as they say 'have mercy on me, a sinner'. But I'll mend my ways, I'm telling you, though it might take quite a little time yet. Ha, Ha, Ha.

SASHA

Do you realise what you are saying? How can you talk such drivel?

KORTOMSKY

Get out, Sasha, shut up Sasha, you're not in the schoolroom now. Some people, I'm telling you, as soon as they open their eyes in the morning, ask: 'what's the weather like? Is the blizzard still blowing? Give me two boiled eggs.' But when Yevstigney Kortomsky wakes up – I'm telling you the first thing he does is to hum tralalalalatata (*hums the first bars of a Mozart fantasia*). Oh, Mozart, oh Bouldieu, music thou art divine! I hear everybody shouting 'The Grand Duke! The Grand Duke!' So naturally, I clean myself up and put on my best clothes. But instead of the Grand Duke, all I see whichever way I look is our Sasha sticking out like a sore thumb.

SASHA

You'd better stop driving those two beggars so hard. They looked after you when you were a child, and we've just seen how disgracefully you treat them. You ought to be ashamed of yourself, sir. And you might turn off that torrent of eloquence. You're only making a nuisance of yourself.

KORTOMSKY

You son of a cat and of a hen! When that dog chewed your father up, it really had you in mind, it just took the wrong piece of meat, I'm telling you.

SASHA

I wasn't even born then, you silly clown!
PROKHOR *walks across down stage and is hidden by the left side of the archway.*

SASHA

(*addressing* DUMAS): That's the man I was telling you about, who is so practical and gifted and resourceful, and who was unjustly sentenced after the Sumtsovo affair. (*Dumas picks up a pencil and notebook, and takes a few steps towards the back of the room. At that moment the entrance door is flung open and several dashing young officers saunter in, their winter greatcoats thrown carelessly over their shoulders. Coachmen and orderlies follow them, carrying travelling bags and trunks.*)

GRAND DUKE

Good day, gentlemen.
The travellers who crowd at the back of the room and are joined by DUMAS, *reply loudly in chorus.*

Voices

Good day, your Imperial Highness!

GENERAL OBLEPIKHIN

Good health to you, gentlemen.

Voices

Good health to your excellency.

OBLEPIKHIN *whispers something to the* GRAND DUKE *who bursts into august and sonorous laughter.*

OBLEPIKHIN

(*to* KUBYNKO): Were you at Sebastopol?

KUBYNKO

Yes, sir.

OBLEPIKHIN

What's your name?

KUBYNKO

Retired Staff Captain Seliverst Kubynko.

OBLEPIKHIN

Where did you lose your leg?

KUBYNKO

In a ravine near Balaclava.

OBLEPIKHIN

Well, you needn't worry, Captain. Your wooden leg carries you along faster than the old one did. One can't keep up with you.

KUBYNKO

That's right sir, I don't worry sir. Glad to be of service, sir.

OBLEPIKHIN

May I report, Your Highness. We can have as many relay horses to Pyatibratskoye as we want, but we've another trouble.

GRAND DUKE

I know, I know, my dear fellow – the road. We'll be held up by snow drifts. Well, we'll have to put up with it.

OBLEPIKHIN

But there's a man here, the hero of many local legends, who keeps an inn. He promises either to put up Your Highness suitably and help you to while away your time, or else to get us this very day to Pyatibratskoye – he says there is no snow drift high enough to hold up his coachmen.

GRAND DUKE

How colourful they are, our self-made people of peasant origin! That must be the man who was sentenced to corporal punishment by mistake – that splendid fellow of an innkeeper they were telling us about on the way, you remember?

The officers are surrounded by an increasingly dense crowd. PROKHOR *joins* SASHA *up stage, and with a confident, experienced movement, draws the curtain which hangs on rings from a rod across the archway.*

PROKHOR

(*to* SASHA): My respects to you. What are you doing here?

SASHA

I was sent to meet a traveller, a French writer.

PROKHOR

Very good, very good.

SASHA

Not at all, it's very bad. Night and day, twenty four hours on end, to keep myself under control, to say yes all the time, to pretend to be what I am not – it's more than flesh and blood can stand. The way the world is organised today, I'd like to put a powder barrel under it, light the fuse and blow it all to smithereens.

PROKHOR

What d'you want to confide in me for, you conspirator? I told you once before, we're not people of the same sort. All right, there was a misfortune. A terrible misfortune you can't put right. Your father was mauled to death by a dog, but does that mean that we must kill off every dog on earth, so that none should be left?

SASHA

What has my father's death got to do with it? You don't understand, Prokhor! I'm talking about the way the whole of life is arranged. These are not simple things. You can't judge of them just like that. You have to think them out. There are long, learned works written about them.

PROKHOR

I know your kind of talk. People who think like you were in prison with me, doing penal servitude. They were always explaining things, I've heard it all over and over again. The Russia of the landowners is ruined and breeds hosts of beggars. But soon the sun will rise. People like me will get their chance, self-made men who get things done and want nothing better than to work. They'll set Russia to rights again. Just wait till after the emancipation, when the peasants have had time to come to their senses, and stand on their own feet. You people can't bear to see anyone get rich by the work of his own hands, and become his own master, and not depend on anybody but himself. As soon as you hear of a man like that you start worrying about his soul. You're afraid he won't want to live in your new godless paradise, the one you've invented, the one you've got out of your books. You're just like the old dissenters[1] turned inside out – you're bigots, scribes and pharisees.

The curtain is drawn back. Through the archway can be seen the officers, KUBYNKO, KSENOFONT, YEVSEY, CHER-NOUSOV, DUMAS, KORTOMSKY, GENERAL OBLE-PIKHIN *and the* GRAND DUKE.

KUBYNKO

Your Highness, this is the man I ventured to tell you about.

GRAND DUKE

Delighted.

To Prokhor.

They've been telling me wonders about you! They say your troikas fly on dragons' wings.

PROKHOR

Wonders are what I deal in, Your Highness. That's my only line of business. Give the order, and you'll be in Pyatibratskoye in a flash.

GRAND DUKE

I wouldn't mind that at all, but I'd like you to give us a meal before we start.

PROKHOR

You'll be served with whatever God has sent. I'm deeply honoured.

---

[1] The Russian word used is *raskolniki.* i.e. Old Believers who did not accept the reform of the Orthodox Church in the 4th century; they were often perse-cuted and tended to be fanatical.

GRAND DUKE

A very bright fellow don't you agree, General?

OBLEPIKHIN

Very bright indeed.

GRAND DUKE

Soon, soon you will unbend your tortured back, soon you will rise to your full stature, our poor, primitive, gifted nation!

KORTOMSKY

Forgive me, Your Imperial Highness, I'm telling you that they're thieves and swindlers, all those simple folk, they're not worthy of your august praise. Nor is that old fox of an inn-keeper Prokhor with his whipped behind. It would be better if, as a member of the happily reigning Imperial family, you, who by your presence have brought light to this backwater of ours, allowed me in my own person . . .

GRAND DUKE

Oh, God, what a bore. Could you get to the point?

KORTOMSKY

To throw myself at your feet as a loyal subject and a spokesman for the genuine aristocracy.

GRAND DUKE

Who are you? How dare you interrupt me and tell me my business?

KORTOMSKY

I have the honour to introduce myself: **Yevstigney Kortomsky,** decayed nobleman reduced to abject vice and ruin by our terrible age of unbelief. I'm telling you.

GRAND DUKE

It's not in the least terrible. I don't agree. On the contrary, it's a wonderful, splendid age, full of radiant promise, a beautiful and fascinating time.

KORTOMSKY

A decayed nobleman fallen on hard times, I'm telling you.

GRAND DUKE

I too am a nobleman, sir, and your nobility does not impress me. Besides which you are an importunate and insolent buffoon. Kindly relieve us of your company. You are in our way and you are making a nuisance of yourself.

To Prokhor.

Now, my good fellow, we'll go across to your house. You'll make room for us under the icons. What is the popular name for a tavern, General?

OBLEPIKHIN

'Under the greenwood bough'.

PROKHOR

That's right, your excellency. It's also called the guest house of the drunken friars.

GRAND DUKE

Always ready with a joke, I see. You've been a soldier, I suppose?

PROKHOR

No, your Highness.

GRAND DUKE

Then how did you get your military bearing?

PROKHOR

In prison. I was driven by way of the green road to Siberia.

GRAND DUKE

Well, that's a sort of training too. You've been through the hands of soldiers after all!

All laugh.